Praise for
FINAL EXIT

"An important indictment of medical practice, legal judgment, and of the culture at large for failing to find a way to protect people against unwanted suffering and lingering death in the company of strangers. . . . This book deserves extensive publicity and consideration for what it means to respect people's choices about dying."

—*American Journal of Law and Medicine*

"Some people want to eke out every second of life—no matter how grim—and that is their right. But others do not. And that should be *their* right."

—Betty Rollin, author of *First, You Cry* and *Last Wish*

"Nobody else could have done this book. It's the first of its kind in America. People in both the present and future will be in Derek Humphry's debt."

—Dr. Joseph F. Fletcher, theologian

"[A]n honest, clear, compelling book for those who seek the knowledge that will assure them a good way through this final passage, should it become necessary."

—Dr. Frederick R. Abrams, physician and ethicist

"No decent human being would allow an animal to suffer without putting it out of its misery. It is only to human beings that human beings are so cruel as to allow them to live on in pain, in hopelessness, in living death, without moving a muscle to help them. It is against such attitudes that this book fights."

—Isaac Asimov

Other books by Derek Humphry

GENERAL
Because They're Black
Passports and Politics
Police Power and Black People
The Cricket Conspiracy
False Messiah

EUTHANASIA
Jean's Way
Let Me Die Before I Wake
The Right to Die
Dying with Dignity
Lawful Exit

FINAL EXIT

The practicalities of self-deliverance and assisted suicide for the dying

Derek Humphry

SECOND EDITION

A Dell Trade Paperback

A DELL TRADE PAPERBACK

Published by
Dell Publishing
a division of
Bantam Doubleday Dell Publishing Group, Inc.
1540 Broadway
New York, New York 10036

Library of Congress Cataloging in Publication Data
Humphry, Derek, 1930–
　　　Final exit: the practicalities of self-deliverance and assisted suicide for the dying / Derek Humphry.—2nd ed.
　　　　　p.　　cm.
　　　"The textbook of euthanasia."
　　　Includes bibliographical references and index.
　　　ISBN 0-440-50785-5 (pbk.)
　　　1. Assisted suicide. 2. Suicide. 3. Euthanasia. I. Title.
R726.H843 1996　　　　　　96-32756
362.2′8—dc20　　　　　　　CIP

Printed in the United States of America

Published simultaneously in Canada

One previous Dell Edition, published September 1992

April 1997

10　9　8　7　6　5　4

BVG

For
Janet Good

AUTHOR'S NOTE

As many of the readers of this book will be people with poor sight, it has been set in large type to assist them. Also, this book assumes the reader's ethical acceptance of the right to choose to die when terminally ill and thus the arguments for and against are not addressed. The history and controversy of this issue can be found in *The Right to Die: Understanding Euthanasia* and *Dying with Dignity*.

Darkling I listen; and, for many a time
I have been half in love with easeful Death,
Call'd him soft names in many a mused rhyme,
To take into the air my quiet breath;
Now more than ever seems it rich to die,
To cease upon the midnight with no pain . . .

John Keats
1795–1821

CONTENTS

Introductions

INTRODUCTION TO THE SECOND EDITION

It is not always easy to die, even when a person is mortally ill and desires a quick end. We have become so brainwashed by the fast, usually bloodless, and always painless deaths shown continually by the movie and television production industry that our collective perceptions of the act of death are sanitized. Whether by gunshot or through illness, the actor just rolls over and that's the end. We want so much to believe that this is true that we don't question it.

I once had the misfortune to see a man shot in the head at point-blank range on a Los Angeles street. Even though he was doomed from the instant the bullet entered his head, he could still cry out, "What have you done?" before collapsing into the storm gutter, where his death throes, lasting several minutes, were pitiful to behold. This is not something you are allowed to see on-screen.

During my twenty years of experience in the right-to-die field, I have heard of plenty of "good deaths"—quick, peaceful, surrounded by love—and also of a few not so good that were characterized by delay, distress for the beholders, and even complete failure. Occasionally patients anxious to die to avoid further suffering woke up a few days later, more often than not in the psychiatric ward of the local hospital.

What separates a chosen "good death" from a bad one almost always comes down, upon analysis, to the amount of planning, attention to detail, and the quality of the assistance, all of which are vital to decent termination of life. These meticulous criteria apply equally to self-deliverance (acting on one's own) and to physician-assisted suicide.

Whether or not a dying person should accelerate the end depends, of course, on the degree of unrelievable suffering involved, his or her conscience, and consideration of the feelings of others. If the reader of this book is deeply religious, and takes all guidance from a divinity, then there is no point in reading further.

All I ask of persons to whom any form of euthanasia is morally repugnant is tolerance and understanding of the feelings of others who want the right to choose what happens to their bodies in a free society. To every person their own way of death.

In its first five years this book was occasionally used by persons for whom it was not intended—the deeply depressed and the mentally ill. This misuse I regret but can do nothing about. Suicide has always been endemic in mankind; some of us do not have the emotional and intellectual equipment to cope with a lifetime of troubles—real and imagined—and elect to die. Self-destruction of a physically fit person is always a tragic waste of life and hurtful to survivors, but life is a personal responsibility. We must each decide for ourselves.

Fortunately, only a tiny portion of Americans commit suicide—approximately 31,000 a year out of an annual death rate of 2,250,000. That statistic has not increased since the publication of this book, but what has happened is that some have chosen their self-destruction by the same methods as the book suggests for the terminally ill. If this means that those individuals bent on suicide for psychological reasons died in a less violent and shocking way than hitherto, then I can live with that. I appeal to all who are thinking of using *Final Exit* as a tool to escape clinical depression or mental illness to first seek medical help and counseling.

I do not think that we yet know enough about the human mind to institute physician-assisted suicide for psychological reasons, although this has been permitted in a few cases in the Netherlands, and I hear other people arguing for it. There is no doubt in my mind that some forms of mental illness are as terrible a torture as unrelieved cancer—and I have a few friends dead by their own hands to prove it. Perhaps escape from their agonies—or, better, a cure—will come in the next century.

My fight since 1976 has been for those adults who desire relief from suffering in the last stages of terminal illness, or

those with an irreversible illness causing protracted and unrelieved suffering. This must be a voluntary, rational request to die, repeated on several occasions, and witnessed
and documented.

When *Final Exit* was first published in early 1991, it
went completely ignored by the media, critics, ethicists—
everybody. Several hundred free copies were circulated to
them, but the old "denial of death" syndrome was in play.
About ten thousand more perceptive members of the Hemlock Society, which I had formed in 1980, purchased the
book in the meantime. Then, in the second half of the year,
a friend in New York interested the *Wall Street Journal* in
the book and the first story about the book was published.
The article said quite bluntly that this was a "how to kill
yourself" book, very controversial, and that some people
strongly disapproved of it. Result: the media detected a hot
controversy, there followed unprecedented publicity, and
Final Exit became an overnight best-seller, spending the
next eighteen weeks on the *New York Times* list of top-
selling books. That fall it was the most talked about book in
America, because the pundits could not fathom why a book
giving guidance on suicide could be in such huge demand.
What, they asked, had happened to America?

The simple answer was perhaps contained in my response
on ABC-TV's "Nightline" program when Barbara Walters
asked me: "Why is it a best-seller, Mr. Humphry?" My
reply was: "Because everybody dies, and nearly every person wonders, however privately, what form that death will
take. They're looking to *Final Exit* for options."

Another answer that I consider valid came from people who asked me to autograph their copy in bookstores. Not a few commented: "This is the best insurance [against a bad death] I've ever bought."

No publisher had the courage to be the first to issue *Final Exit* in the United States, Australia, or Britain, so I published it myself using the financial backing of my organization, the Hemlock Society, which turned out lucky for Hemlock because it netted for them nearly one million dollars in profits that otherwise might have gone to a commercial publisher.

Once the taboo against having the ultimate "how-to" book available in stores and libraries was smashed, other publishers rushed in. It is now on sale through normal book trade channels throughout the English-speaking world, and can be read in all the world's major languages in eleven different translations.

Most of the money the book earned for Hemlock has subsequently been used to help fund citizens' ballot initiatives in Washington State (1991), California (1992), and Oregon (1994). The first two initiatives sought legalization of both active voluntary euthanasia and physician-assisted suicide. Both lost narrowly, gaining 46 percent of the vote, due to strong resistance just prior to the election by the Christian religious right. (In California, 46 percent of the votes cast was 4.5 million—hardly a minority. Often Presidents are elected by smaller percentages.)

Reviewing the first two defeats, Oregon changed tactics and sought voter approval for a lesser law permitting physician-assisted suicide (in which a doctor provides lethal drugs that a patient consumes) and that specifically excluded any form of euthanasia (death by medical injection). Despite determined resistance from the mainstream churches, this law scraped through with 51 percent of the vote.

Some hold that success came this time because of the narrower scope of the bill, but I believe the victory was due to timing. The voters had been educated and had become accustomed to the idea of lawful assisted death through the massive publicity accorded the brave Michigan doctor Jack Kevorkian, to the breakthrough into bookstores and libraries of *Final Exit,* and to another gutsy but more mainstream physician, Timothy Quill, in New York State. Dr. Quill revealed in a prestigious medical journal that not only did he believe in assisted suicide in certain circumstances but that he had also practiced it.

The Oregon law did not take effect because the National Right to Life Committee, branching out from its usual occupation of trying to stop women from having legal abortions, secured a court injunction blocking its implementation. A single judge accepted their arguments that the law was unconstitutional, but this decision is being energetically appealed to higher courts.

Ballot initiatives and court cases were not the only attempts to reform the law on assisted death. Between 1990 and 1996, sixteen American state legislatures considered bills permitting physician-assisted suicide. None of them passed, but all are likely to be reintroduced again and again until they do. Groundbreaking social reform like this in the face of institutional opposition requires persistence.

To most people's surprise, the next place to tackle the euthanasia issue was the Northern Territories of Australia in 1995. This state is more famous for its huge jungles and its crocodiles than for social-reform zeal. The law, passed by the state's elected representatives, approves both voluntary euthanasia and assisted suicide for the terminally ill, and took effect in July 1996.

The world's testing laboratory for all forms of euthanasia is, of course, the Netherlands. Step by careful step since 1973, the Dutch medical profession, lawyers, thinkers, and politicians have been creating the guidelines for compassionate, justifiable assisted death. Detailed surveys, studies, and reports pour out from Holland to steer the rest of us over the rocky shores of this new and complex procedure.

Opponents of euthanasia frequently claim that accelerated death deprives the patient and family of the loving relationships, closure, and the peace of a natural death. They make this claim in total ignorance of the circumstances of elective deaths, which can be, and usually are, just as fulfilling as theirs, perhaps more so because the dying person has said, "This is the time that I die." Through honest acceptance of the inevitability of death, and arranging its timing, family and friends can come openly to say their last good-byes and the needed thank-yous.

The other right-to-life canard is that believers in self-determination will kill themselves immediately when they learn they have a terminal illness. In fact, right-to-die supporters love life as much as anybody and hold on until the last moment, sometimes—so I've witnessed—too long, then lose control of the situation.

Frequently I am asked if I will take my life when I have a terminal illness. My answer is: "I'll wait and see." If my dying is bearable, the pain being well managed, and my self-control and dignity are not damaged, then I shall hang on and die naturally. But if I am one of the unlucky few who suffer abysmally, then I shall make a quick exit. This book is intended for readers who think much the same as me.

While it is true that I built my reputation as a leading figure in the right-to-die movement at the same time that I started and constructed the Hemlock Society, I retired from that organization in 1992. It had become a huge administrative chore. In the autumn of my life I prefer to be a communicator rather than an organizational executive.

Today I work as a volunteer full-time for the movement, writing, lecturing, and running a small information organization, the Euthanasia Research and Guidance Organization (ERGO!). If you are ever placed in a position where you need to take your life in the circumstances outlined in this introduction, and there is something important still puzzling you about the technique, feel free to contact ERGO! for a discussion. Details on how to reach ERGO! can be found at the back of this book, which you must first have read carefully—perhaps twice—for a good death requires courage, support, and strict attention to details. Enjoy the rest of your life!

—Derek Humphry
Eugene, Oregon
August 1996

INTRODUCTION TO THE FIRST EDITION

When my first wife could no longer bear the pain and deterioration of her body and the distressed quality of her life from cancer, she asked me to help her end her life. It was both a logical and a poignant request.

But what should I do? I was not a doctor or a pharmacist. Violent ending of life, such as shooting, stabbing, or strangling, was deeply abhorrent to me, largely because my thirty-five years as a newspaper reporter had too often shown me the ugly end results.

"Find a doctor who will give us a lethal overdose that I can take," Jean pleaded. Unable to bear to see her suffering and noting the calmness of her request, I decided, then and there, to help.

Who could I ask? The three doctors who had been treating her with great skill and dedication came to mind first. They had spent so much time caring for her, although they now recognized—and spoke openly to her and to me—that death was approaching, and that they were running out of countermeasures.

However, I was thinking of asking one of these three highly professional men to commit a crime: that of assisting a suicide. The penal code takes no account of a person's wish to die, nor of how close and inevitable death may be. If it were discovered that one of them had helped my wife to die, that individual would be subject to prosecution in court, and disqualification from practicing medicine.

I couldn't ask them, I decided. But I still had to help Jean—she was depending on me.

Then I remembered a young doctor whom I had met many years before while reporting on medical matters for my newspaper.

I called "Dr. Joe" and asked if we could meet. He invited me to his consulting rooms, for he had by now become an eminent physician with a lucrative practice. As prestigious and powerful as he was, he still had not lost the compassion and humanity that I had noted in earlier years. I told him how seriously ill Jean was and of her desire to die soon. He questioned me closely about the state of the disease, its effects on her, and what treatments she had undergone.

As soon as he heard that some of her bones were breaking at the slightest sudden movement, he stopped the conversation. "There's no quality of life left for her," he said. He got up from his desk and strode to his medicine cabinet.

Dr. Joe did some mixing of pills, and handed a vial to me. He explained that the capsules should be emptied into a sweet drink to reduce the bitter taste.

"This is strictly between you and me," he said, looking straight into my eyes.

"You have my word that no one will ever know of your part in this," I promised. I thanked him and left.

A few weeks later, when Jean knew the time had come, she asked me for the drugs. As wrenching as it was, I had to agree. We spent the morning reminiscing about our twenty-two years together. Then, after dissolving the pills in some coffee, we said our last good-byes. I watched as Jean picked up the coffee and drank it down. She barely had time to murmur, "Good-bye, my love," before falling asleep. Fifty minutes later she stopped breathing.

My wife died in 1975 as she wished and as she deserved. However, to accomplish that, two crimes were committed.

First, Dr. Joe broke the law by prescribing drugs for a patient not registered with him, a patient he had never seen. Also, he had assisted a suicide because he handed over the drugs knowing what they were intended for.

Second, I committed the crime of assisting a suicide, the penalty for which in Britain, where I was living at the time, is up to fourteen years imprisonment. (Although this incident happened in England, it could as well have happened in America, where I now live, because the laws in the United States and all Western countries on this issue are almost exactly the same. The penalty in California, for example, is five years.)

Now, did Dr. Joe and I commit truly felonious, culpable

crimes and did we deserve punishment? Aren't these archaic laws ready to be changed to situations befitting modern understanding and morality?

Not everybody has as good a friend in the medical profession as I had. Moreover, why should caring doctors like Dr. Joe have to take such appalling risks?

Had I broken down when interviewed by detectives about Jean's death and revealed Dr. Joe's identity, he would have been prosecuted and professionally ruined. There are other cases in which that has happened. Also, there was the hypocrisy of how it all turned out.

The authorities only learned of the manner of Jean's death from my 1978 biography of her, *Jean's Way*. The book caused such a stir they felt obliged to interrogate me. When the police came to talk to me, I immediately confessed to them and offered to plead guilty at any trial. But, a few months later I received a note from the public prosecutor: he had decided not to charge me.

The taboo on suicide for reasons of health has been broken since 1980. It is now recognized that elder suicide is widespread and, while it may need to be addressed in terms of social and health care policy, it does not deserve spontaneous condemnation. There is evidence of considerable public—and legal—sympathy for mercy killers, those desperate people who unilaterally kill their loved ones in the belief that it is the only compassionate thing to do. Intellectual giants such as Arthur Koestler, Sigmund Freud, and Bruno Bettelheim chose to end their lives and did not meet the storm of shock and criticism occasioned by Pitney Van

Dusen, the theologian, after his self-deliverance from terminal old age in 1975.

When Dr. Jack Kevorkian chose in 1990 to help Janet Adkins commit suicide in the early stages of Alzheimer's disease, despite some criticism by a few psychologists and self-styled ethicists, there was tremendous public support evidenced for his compassion.

The time is not far off when physician-assisted suicide in justifiable cases will be lawful in enlightened countries. The euthanasia societies in the Netherlands, Britain, France, and the United States are currently finding their law reform proposals much more acceptable to the public, the medical and legal professionals, and the politicians. The Hemlock movement in America has made significant political progress on the West Coast, particularly in the states of Washington and Oregon.

I first published my book on self-deliverance, *Let Me Die Before I Wake,* independently in 1981. No mainstream publisher would touch it. Despite a hail of criticisms and hypocritical commentary, it sold well (more than 130,000 copies) and countless hundreds of people have used it as an informational aid to end lives which, for medical reasons, were unbearable to them. There may have been abuse of the book—when a product is available to some 300 million people in North America, nobody can verify the reasons for every death—but misuse has yet to be documented. In its updated version, *Let Me Die Before I Wake* continues to find readers because it deals with self-deliverance as it affects the individual and the family. In that respect it is timeless.

Now is the time to go one step further. *Final Exit: The Practicalities of Self-deliverance and Assisted Suicide for the Dying* is a book for the 1990s. As a society we have moved on. People today are remarkably well informed about medical problems through television, magazines, and books. Personal autonomy concerning one's bodily integrity has taken hold in the public imagination. Most people have an opinion regarding the situations of Nancy Cruzan, Karen Ann Quinlan, Roswell Gilbert, and other right-to-die celebrity cases. Physicians are now more likely to be seen as "friendly body technicians" and no longer as the rulers of one's bodily health whose every piece of advice must be interpreted as a command.

Final Exit is aimed at helping the public and the health professional achieve death with dignity for those who desire to plan for it.

—Derek Humphry
Eugene, Oregon
December 1990

CAUTION

If you are thinking of ending your life because you are depressed, or cannot cope with the pressures of this difficult world, do not use this book. It is for dying individuals who need such information and will find it a great solace.

I ask people with suicidal thoughts to share them with family or friends and if this does not help to call one of the hot lines or help lines listed in their local telephone book, and presented in Appendix D of this book.

Please respect the true intentions of *Final Exit:* the right of a terminally ill person with unbearable suffering to know how to choose to die.

This book is not intended as a substitute for legal advice of attorneys. The reader should consult an attorney with regard to questions of a legal nature.

1

The Most Difficult Decision

This is the scenario: You are terminally ill, all medical treatments acceptable to you have been exhausted, and the suffering in its different forms is unbearable. Because the illness is serious, you recognize that your life is drawing to a close. Euthanasia comes to mind as a way of release.

The dilemma is awesome. But it has to be faced. Should you battle on, take the pain, endure the indignity, and await the inevitable end, which may be days, weeks, or months away? Or should you take control of the situation and resort to some form of euthanasia, which in its modern-language definition has come to mean "help with a good death"?

Today the euthanasia option—or the right to choose to die—comes in four ways:

Passive euthanasia. Popularly known as "pulling the plug," it is the disconnection of medical life-support equipment without which you cannot live. It could be a respirator to aid breathing, a feeding tube to provide liquids and nutrition, or even the sophisticated use of certain drugs to stave off death. There is not likely to be much ethical or legal trouble here provided that you have signed a Living Will and also a Durable Power of Attorney for Health Care—they are also known as Advance Declarations—that express your wishes. (More on these later.)

Self-deliverance. Taking your own life to escape the suffering. This method does not involve any other person directly, although a loved one or friend should ideally be present. It is legal in all respects, and widely accepted ethically.

Assisted suicide. You get lethal drugs from somebody else, usually a physician, and swallow them to cause your death. It is legal for you to do so, but at present it is a felony for the person who supplied the drugs or took any action physically to help you. Despite the present criminality of assistance, this procedure is gaining increasing ethical acceptance. In 1996 two U.S. appeal courts ruled in favor of physician-assisted suicide, making it likely that this is the modified form of assisted death which will be adopted.

Active euthanasia. Death brought about by a physician's injection of lethal drugs. This procedure is illegal and, despite the necessity for it in certain cases, has limited ethical acceptance. It is already available in the Netherlands and parts of Australia but is probably more distant in America.

Often, persons who have not properly thought these situations through claim they are not worried about a bad death because they have a Living Will and the plug can be pulled at their behest. Probably so, but roughly half the people who die in Western society are not connected to life-support equipment in their final days, so relief by that way is not an option.

Before we go any further, let me say this: If you consider the God whom you worship to be the absolute master of your fate, then read no more. Seek the best pain management available and arrange for hospice care.

If you want personal control and choice over your final exit, it will require forethought, planning, documentation, good friends, and decisive, courageous action by you. This book will help in many ways, but in the last analysis, whether you bring your life to a quick end, and how you achieve this, is entirely your responsibility, ethically and legally.

The task of finding the right drugs, getting someone to help or at least be with you, and carrying out your exit in a place and in a manner that is not upsetting to other people is your task. Suicide, even the most rational and justified version, the sort we are talking about in this book, is not something other people are anxious to be involved in. It is best to seek the help of family or the closest of friends.

If you have not already done so, sign a Living Will and

have it witnessed, but not by anybody who is going to gain from your other will dealing with your estate. A Living Will, which has nothing to do with property or money, is an advance declaration of your wish not to be connected to life-support equipment if it is judged that you are hopelessly and terminally ill.

Or, if you are already on the equipment because of an attempt to save you that has failed, a Living Will gives permission for its disconnection. By signing, you are agreeing to accept the fatal consequences.

Make sure you get the particular Living Will form that is relevant to your state. They all differ in small details. Strictly speaking, the Living Will of one state or nation does not apply in another place. But carry it when you are away from home, because any sensible physician would recognize it as a valid statement of your wishes. A valid Living Will is likely to survive a court challenge because all American states recognize them and the U.S. Supreme Court has given them its blessing.

But remember this: A Living Will is only a *request* to a doctor that you not be kept needlessly alive on support equipment. It is not an order. It may not be legally enforceable. But as your signed "release" of his or her responsibility, it can be a valuable factor in the doctor's thinking about how to handle your last hours. The Living Will gives the doctor a measure of protection from lawsuits by relatives after your death. And it gives you a measure of control and choice.

A more powerful document is the Durable Power of Attorney for Health Care, which, in different forms, is available in all American states. Here you assign to someone else the power to make health care decisions if and when you cannot.

For example, if your doctor is unable to make you understand the consequences of what treatment or care is planned, then he or she will turn to the next of kin; you are considered incompetent. Now, if the family member is confused, or has different ethical values than you, that may not work well. You may end up getting medical attention of the sort you did not want when you were rational.

With the medical Power of Attorney given to someone in whom you have already confided your general or specific wishes, someone who has accepted the responsibility, then it is most likely that you will get the kind of treatment—or dignified death—that you desire. A doctor must get the approval of the person (also known as surrogate or attorney-in-fact) that you have named. This is especially important if there is disagreement in the family about what to do. The surrogate person has the absolute right to make the final decision, although only if you are too ill to make it yourself.

The medical Power of Attorney is legally enforceable, whereas the Living Will is not. It may seem like a man using both a belt and braces to keep his trousers up, but experience shows that if you care about a good death you cannot be too careful.

The Durable Power of Attorney for Health Care could be the most significant document you ever sign. As of today, however, it works only for passive euthanasia—the cessation of treatment. It does not empower anybody to assist in your suicide or provide euthanasia. Since 1991 the Patient

Self-Determination Act, passed by Congress, requires all federally funded hospitals in the United States to advise patients of their right to make out any Advance Declarations their state has. Some hospitals supply this information efficiently; others do not. So it is absolutely necessary for you to sign these documents when you are healthy and get copies into your medical files, your private files, with your attorney if you have one, and with the person who is to be your surrogate decision-maker. Also, hand copies to some or all of your adult children.

This book is chiefly about self-deliverance, assisted suicide, and euthanasia, which the Advance Declarations do not cover. But undoubtedly the very existence of two properly signed declarations would influence health care workers if a question of hastening a death arose. Membership in a right-to-die organization, and having read this book, are at present the two most powerful demonstrations a person can make of sincere beliefs in assisted dying.

Where do you get the documents? From a good stationery store, your primary-care physician, local hospital, or call the state medical society. Nowadays most attorneys, when drawing up your financial will, will ask if you also would like Advance Declarations. This service is worth a few dollars extra. You could also call Choice in Dying in New York City, at 1-800-989-WILL.

A Warning

Some lawyers and concerned groups advocate signing an Advance Declaration that contains many caveats and conditions under which they may take effect, a whole "laundry list" of your medical provisos so that every possible illness is embraced. This seemed a good idea at first, putting in writing which medical conditions were important to you and under what medical state you wanted to be allowed to die. But experience has shown one serious flaw in the "I want this and I don't want that" type of Advance Declarations. What if you are dying of a condition not mentioned in your document? It is impossible to think of every possible way in which death may come. Disputes have arisen between hospitals and patient-surrogates because a particular illness or injury was not spelled out in the document, whereas many others not relevant to the patient were.

My advice is to use those Advance Declarations that your state has approved which make simple and broad statements to the effect that you do not want "heroic measures" carried out merely to keep you alive in a clearly terminal condition. It is a mistake to think that these Advance Declarations are absolutely foolproof: academic studies have shown that many doctors either are ignorant of them or disregard them. To get them respected it is sometimes necessary to be noisy and threatening. Tell the doctor or hospital executive who is being uncooperative that your lawyer will be in touch with them tomorrow to initiate a lawsuit. That usually wakes them up to their responsibilities.

Once these documents are completed, you are ready to plan and tackle the other aspects of bringing your life to an end if and when the suffering in your view justifies it.

2

Shopping for the Right Doctor

If you are interested in the option of assisted dying at life's end, good rapport with your doctor is extremely useful. It is important that your doctor know your views on dying and death so that he or she is forewarned. This way there will be one believable witness around who can testify to a rational decision made well before health problems became critical and distracting. This may influence possible inquiries later on by the police and coroner's office.

Therefore, unless you are perfectly satisfied with your present doctor, and both of you are on the same ethical wavelengths regarding issues of death and dying, you should now shop around for another.

Have you directly tested your present doctor's views on right-to-die issues? Don't take any chances. Just because a doctor is a nice person, appearing to be very caring, does not automatically mean that you share religious views and cultural values. Find out. The perfect opening gambit to test views on passive euthanasia (allowing to die) is to arrive at the doctor's office with your completed Living Will and Durable Power of Attorney for Health Care. Present these documents and candidly ask if they will be respected when the time comes for you to die.

One way to ask the next question about assisted suicide would be to say, "Doctor, you've heard they've passed a law in Oregon allowing physician-assisted suicide under certain conditions. If that was law here, would you help me to die?" With the question framed this way, you are not going to embarrass the doctor by asking if he or she would break the law for you.

Make your own careful judgment from the answers you receive as to whether this is the right doctor for you. Do not be influenced by kindly and well-meant remarks such as "Don't worry. I won't let you suffer," or "Leave it to me. I've never let a patient die in pain." This sort of response is too vague and general to be relied upon. It may only mean that you'll be "snowed" with narcotic drugs for the last days of life if they happen to be extremely painful. (That "knockout" procedure, known as "barbiturate sedation," may be acceptable to you. Fine. But some of us want to be able to say good-bye to the world in a manner of our choosing.)

Pin the doctor down. Would life-support equipment be disconnected once it was realized that there was no hope of recovery? Would such equipment be used regardless of a prognosis of hopeless terminal illness? Having opened up the subject with these basic (and legal) questions, then address the matters where the law unfortunately is less clear. Tell the doctor that you have read this book, that you are a supporter of a particular right-to-die group (if you are), and ask directly if lethal drugs would be supplied to you in certain compassionate, terminal circumstances.

The doctor's reply to this tough line of questioning may be an outright rejection on religious or legal grounds. Or it may be hedged because of the complications of the current laws, or ignorance of them. The doctor does not want to be trapped. Today more and more doctors—particularly the younger ones—have taken the trouble to read and think about euthanasia. Thus, a few will give you an outright assurance of direct help should it be needed eventually. The number of doctors who think progressively on this subject today amounts, surveys show, to at least 50 percent, so there is hope that your approach will be well received.

You have to judge from the nature of the answers to your questions whether this is the doctor for you. Of course, if the Advance Declarations are scorned, or there is ignorance of them on the part of the doctor, you need to change immediately.

Call your local hospitals and ask for their physician-referral service. If that doesn't work, look up the medical society of your county or state in the telephone book and call them. Get the names and numbers of five or six doctors who are reasonably close to you; also, if you have any particular health problem, ask for their specialties. And don't forget to check with your health insurance company on whether these doctors are on their acceptance list.

Call ahead and make appointments with these doctors, saying that you would like about twenty minutes of their time for a "get to know each other" session. You will find that most will appreciate your investigations; the medical profession is a lot less stuffy and formal than it used to be.

Speaking for myself, at age sixty-six, I tend to choose a doctor in the 40s age range, male or female, in general preference to an older one. My observations of and contacts with hundreds of doctors, both in my journalistic and right-to-die careers, indicate that younger physicians are less dogmatic and self-opinionated. They understand the full implications of modern medical technology a great deal better than their elders, are more open to new ideas, and usually are keenly aware of today's medical controversies, including law and ethics.

While you are waiting to see the doctor for this mutual selection interview, assess the appearance of the waiting room and such things as whether the magazines are changed regularly. Are the staff pleasant and helpful? Here are the clues to the level of consideration given to the patients. You do not want a doctor who is merely running a business! If you are kept waiting some time—and this happens in medical emergencies—observe whether the doctor apologizes for the delay and at least hints at the reason why.

Be quick to put the doctor at ease. You start the talking. Tell who you are, where you live, and what your health priorities will be. Be candid about why you are changing doctors—he or she will pick it up in the professional gossip anyway. It might only be that you have changed residence. Briefly describe any medical problem you have. After getting responses, bring up the Living Will matters, followed by the more critical issue of how you might want to die when the time comes.

Don't be nervous about asking the doctor for some objective criteria. How long has the doctor been in medicine and where did his or her qualification as a physician take place? At which hospital or hospitals does the doctor have privileges? Does this doctor do the in-hospital supervision of patients or does one of his or her partners? Is this doctor a board-certified specialist in any particular branch of medicine? It is obviously very important to ask that arrangements be made to transfer your old medical records to the new doctor. There should be no trouble with this—provided you are leaving no unpaid bills behind—but should there be complications ask your state health department or your attorney for help.

It is best not to sign up with any doctor on the spot. Go home and think about your research. Talk it over with your spouse or companion if you have one, because when you are ill, it is often they who must communicate a great deal with the doctor. Share your thoughts about the various doctors before coming to a decision.

When you have made your choice, find out which hospital that doctor most uses for admitting patients. This hospital might have a preadmission procedure. Some even promote this feature with a tour of the facilities and free lunches. If possible, get copies of your Living Will and Durable Power of Attorney for Health Care filed with the hospital in advance. (You will by now, of course, have filed them with your doctor.) If your medical records have no recent activity, they could be lost or filed away forgotten, so it is a wise precaution to take them with you on the first hospital admission you might have.

Until tested by serious problems, "in the line of fire" so to speak, you cannot make a perfect assessment of any doctor. The best you can do while "shopping around" is to locate the one with whom you communicate well and who seems to have broadly the same ethics as you. That is a big start.

3

Beware of the Law

Taking one's own life is not a crime—it used to be in some places until the 1960s—but helping another person to die is presently against the law in America. Assistance in suicide has never been against the law in Switzerland, Uruguay, Norway, and Germany provided the circumstances were provably compassionate and justifiable. You would be unwise to think of going to one of those countries, because they do not like strangers taking advantage of their laws. Also, the complications of your medical care and insurance would be horrendous.

The voters of the state of Oregon voted in November 1994 in favor of a law permitting physician-assisted suicide (Ballot Measure 16), but it was immediately blocked in the courts by the National Right to Life Committee, and whether it will become law may not be known for some time. The Dutch officially permit voluntary euthanasia and physician-assisted suicide provided guidelines are observed, but these acts remain a crime if the rules are not obeyed. In February 1995, elected representatives of the Northern Territories area of Australia voted in favor of medically assisted dying, and this came into effect in July 1996.

In these three places it is the *doctor* who, within certain guidelines, may help a terminally ill person to die. In the Netherlands and the Northern Territories the doctor can use either a direct injection or prescribe the drugs that the patient takes. In the Oregon law—if and when it takes effect—a doctor may only prescribe drugs. No injections are permitted. Only residents of the state are eligible.

These three laws are the "foot in the door" we need to get beneficent and legal euthanasia, but they are highly controversial and subject to change. Oregon's voters may not see their wishes obeyed for several years, and not at all if the U.S. Supreme Court happens to rule that laws providing physician-assisted suicide are unconstitutional. My guess is that it will not, but at the time of writing we must wait and see.

Assisted-suicide bills have been before sixteen American states in recent years. All but two—Maine's and New Hampshire's—died in committee stages. On the floor of the legislatures, enough politicians in Maine and New Hampshire lacked the compassion and courage to make it law in their state.

Where does this leave the people who want assistance in suicide to escape intolerable suffering? And how do people who help stand? Answer: on their own. But there are ways in which self-deliverance and assisted dying can take place without jeopardizing anybody. One needs to be keenly aware of this particular law and how it is enforced (if at all).

First, it is not a crime in America to watch somebody kill themselves and do nothing to stop it. (It may be in some other countries, but this is untested and thus unclear.) Therefore, a person can give the dying patient the absolutely essential gift of being present at the deathbed because (a) nobody should have to die alone; and (b) the presence of a caring friend reduces the chance of the self-deliverance being botched. In nearly every case in which I hear of a failed self-deliverance, the dying person has acted alone. (More on this later.) There are a few people who tell me that they are so used to a solitary life that they will die alone, but even here I advise them that if they are thinking of self-deliverance the chances of the action not being botched are much better if a friend is present.

About half the states of America have a specific law forbidding assistance in suicide, and the other half could prosecute under general homicide statutes. No defense that this was a genuine case of physical suffering, or that there was a written request, is permitted.

Bertram Harper found this out to his cost when he flew with his terminally ill wife from California to Michigan in the summer of 1990, thinking he would be able to help her die without fear of prosecution. At that time Michigan had no legal prohibition on assisted suicide, which was why Dr. Jack Kevorkian operated with legal impunity for some time. Mr. Harper openly told Detroit police that he had helped his wife die by affixing a plastic bag, thinking he was in the clear, and they promptly charged him with first-degree murder. At his trial the next year a spirited defense team pleaded that he had acted out of love, I gave evidence of how his misunderstanding of the law came about, and he went into the witness box to defend himself. The jury acquitted him. But the moral of Harper's experience is: If you have to help a person die, say nothing. Let the police do their own sleuthing.

The cardinal rules for helping a loved one or dear friend die lie in the answers to these questions:

1. In terms of your personal philosophy and ethics, is this the right thing to do? Are you comfortable with it in your conscience?
2. Is your relationship with the person who is asking for help one of love, loyalty, and respect? If the connection between you is anything less, do not help. This is too serious a matter for a poor, a casual, or a brief relationship.
3. If by chance the law-enforcement authorities find out you helped, are you prepared to take the consequences, whatever they may be?
4. Who else knows or might get to know about this intended action, and will they keep it secret? Beware of a deeply religious person, particularly one who is

"born again," within the family who might cause trouble.

What does "assisted the suicide" mean in this context?

Assisting in dying could simply mean being present during the happening, and giving love and moral support to the act. There is no illegality in that, as I have said. In my credo, having somebody present at this time when a person is carrying out their final exit is absolutely essential. Isolation at such a time is an inhuman experience.

Never, ever join in the slightest attempt to persuade a dying person to hasten the end. Rather, argue gently and reasonably against such action, seeking alternatives, testing the will of the patient. But do not be obdurate; if the dying person is exploring the act of self-deliverance, then she or he needs you as a sounding board. Many laws are specific about the criminality of "counseling and procuring" a suicide. In any event, it is ethically a wrong thing to do.

Providing information about how persons may end their life is not a crime, at least in the United States, or I would have spent the last fifteen years behind bars! The law is not so clear in Britain, where the Voluntary Euthanasia Society in London decided in 1983 to withdraw its *Guide to Self-Deliverance* pamphlet after lawyers warned of possible prosecutions. This made British publishers leery of publishing *Final Exit,* but I made arrangements in 1991 for the American edition to be shipped in via normal trade channels and it sold freely in bookstores without hindrance. It is my belief that the book benefited from a climate of tolerance to the subject matter, which meant the prosecutors looked the other way. *Final Exit* remains banned by law in France, but attempted official bannings in Australia and New Zealand failed on appeal.

Experience since the 1991 publication shows that it helps to leave a copy of *Final Exit* at the bedside of the dead person who has used it. This immediately sends a signal to the authorities that "it's one of those euthanasia suicides" (their description). Mark certain passages in the book and sign it with your name.

Actually supplying the means—drugs, plastic bags, elastic bands, etc.—may well be a crime, although here again there are no clear court examples to confirm that it is so. What authorities generally look for is *evidence of intent.* By that they mean *evil intent.* They are less likely to prosecute if your motives are always pure and justifiable. Act with caution and discretion.

Touching the person in the act of helping him or her to die is where criminal liability is possible. Giving an injection, holding the cup to the mouth, helping to put a plastic bag over the head and securing it—all are actions that prosecutors could use to enforce existing laws against assistance in dying. In a 1996 assisted-suicide case in Missouri the prosecutor charged the family with voluntary manslaughter, citing the moving of furniture to make it easier for the old lady to get at her drugs, buying the orange juice in which they were dissolved, turning down the heat so that she was cooler, reading aloud to her portions of *Final Exit*—anything to get a conviction. Fortunately for her helpers, the case collapsed.

So as to avoid possible trouble with the law, here are the basic rules:

1. Don't persuade the dying person; up to a point try to dissuade with reason.
2. Don't touch. It must be self-deliverance. Don't physically assist.
3. If you must touch because the patient is physically helpless—amyotrophic lateral sclerosis (ALS) might be the most common example—absolute silence both before and after the death is paramount. You must not tell anyone about this.
4. Give comfort and love, and provide privacy and security.
5. Do not dial 911 for the emergency services. That immediately activates paramedics who will try to revive the person, and policemen who are looking for something to do, especially if it is out of the ordinary. Call only the doctor and ask for a death certificate.
6. Make sure that the person being helped has left a note in their handwriting giving their reasons for self-deliverance and accepting personal responsibility.
7. Before and after, say nothing to anybody. If the police want to ask lots of questions, answer only in the presence of a lawyer. Do not assume you are in the clear; that has trapped many people.

Should you be subsequently asked questions by anybody, state quietly and emphatically that you were close to the dead person, gave them no encouragement to die, you did not touch, and were merely present as an observer because you enjoyed a close relationship.

Laws exist to prevent abuse of normal, civilized behavior. If your assistance in helping to ease the suffering of a person who could bear no more was a loving act, and justifiable in human terms, then your conscience is clear.

". . . the rest is silence," as Hamlet said as he died.

4

The Hospice Option

"Don't even consider euthanasia," a friend might say. "Think about a hospice." Certainly. There are two types of hospice care: inpatient and home. In America you are unlikely to be offered a bed in a hospice unit, because there are very few. In Britain and France, a bed is a distinct possibility in difficult medical cases. Because of population size, distance, and finance, the United States has had to organize home hospice programs where the doctors and nurses care for the patient through frequent visits.

Sometimes patients are in hospitals or other health care facilities and still get hospice care on-call by visiting doctors and nurses. The most recent survey figures (1991) show that America had 951 hospices that year which helped

43,487 patients. (More than two million people die in the United States every year.)

Hospices provide the best in pain management and comfort care. They are skilled in the sophisticated use of modern drugs to alleviate pain, while still in many cases keeping the patient conscious most of the time. They have developed remarkable ways to alleviate the symptoms of terminal illness, which are many, and often are more distressing than the effects of the actual illness.

One of the most valuable services that hospice care offers is respite from the continual burden of care for the family member or members looking after a dying person. A hospice may be able to provide someone for several days, nights, or a week, to enable a stressed-out caregiver to take a break.

What these services all boil down to is good and appropriate medical and social care for the dying. All good hospitals have now adopted the hospice model of care for their dying patients. It is interesting to note that Scandinavian countries do not permit hospices to start up—for them pain management and good home care are part of the total medical package provided by the health service.

To enter a hospice program, you and/or your family have to agree with the treating doctors that death is likely to come within the next six months. Nowadays most health insurance programs cover hospice expenses—it's cheaper for them than the patient being in an acute-care hospital. There will be no life-support equipment, such as respirators or artificial-feeding gadgets, available.

In a hospice program you will not be helped to die in any

deliberate manner, so there is no point in asking. Not that some hospice patients don't ask for an accelerated death. One survey of 331 hospice patients showed that 12 percent of them asked the hospice staff to help with a quick death. It did not happen. I was told of one instance where a hospice patient had a copy of *Final Exit* and it was eagerly passed from bed to bed like a best-selling thriller novel!

The leadership of the hospice movement constantly insists that it has complete answers to painful dying and that there is absolutely no need for any form of euthanasia. But evidence has come forward from some experienced doctors and nurses that the situation is not as rosy as that. While hospices do relieve the majority of pain and give wonderful comfort care, there are still a number of distressing cases, about 10 percent of the total.

For instance, a highly qualified hospice nurse, Theresa M. Stephany, RN, MS, CRNH, CS, writing in the *American Journal of Hospice and Palliative Care* (July/August 1994, Vol. 2 No. 4) said: "It is insulting to assume that patients who request assisted suicide are clinically depressed. Most are just realistic. They know what lies ahead and they'd rather not continue with it. Let's be honest: despite our best efforts, some deaths are simply too horrible to believe." (I'll spare you the very gory details that she sets out in the article.)

This nurse, at the end of her article, makes a very interesting point that serves as a warning to readers of this book: "Despite its rhetoric and good intentions, today's hospice care does not provide what many patients are genuinely seeking—a voice in the type of help they want." If you are interested in having control over your care and your death, consider carefully whether a hospice is the route for you. Of course, home hospice care does not rule out the individual option of self-deliverance as the end approaches.

Some hospices are run by religious orders. Others are run by local groups and medical professionals out of humanitarian motives. Eighty-eight percent of hospices are nonprofit, 5 percent are commercial, and 6 percent are governmental. Between 60 and 70 percent are Medicare and Medicaid certified, so check on this as well in case the one near you happens not to be.

If you enter a hospice unit run by a religious order, you may find regular prayers being said in your presence. This might please or displease you, so find out in advance.

Hospice leaders frequently insist that it is *fear* of pain that propels people into thinking about euthanasia. They claim they can control all pain. They can even do so in extreme cases by dosing the patients so heavily with narcotic analgesics (opium-based painkillers), or by barbiturate sedation (powerful sleep aids), that the patient is unconscious for the final days before death. If that form of death is acceptable to you, then hospice is your route of choice.

But some of us want our final days to be dignified and be able to say good-bye to our friends and the world we have enjoyed. Being "put under" is a sort of cop-out. Of course we don't want pain, and in 90 percent of cases that can be relieved. If we are in the 10 percent, then some of us want the means and the option to check out quickly.

It is this "quality of life" argument that hospice leaders find hard to accept. While a hospice does its wonderful best to control the symptoms of terminal illness—constipation, sleeplessness, dry mouth, bedsores, to name but a few—accounts from patients show that they do not have all the answers in every case.

Hospice leaders argue that the final days and hours of a dying person are invariably an opportunity for love and closure with family and friends. But that argument assumes that pro-euthanasia people kill themselves early and do not enjoy such familial pleasures. My experience from knowing hundreds of cases is that when self-deliverance or assisted suicide is carried out, there is almost always the same late-stage, significant family reunion and closure. In fact, the closure in a case of accelerated, date-fixed dying is more effective and poignant because everybody concerned knows in advance that the patient will be gone at a preordained time.

Both a hospice and euthanasia provide invaluable services to different types of people with many varying ethics and a range of medical problems. It's a matter of choice.

For information about hospice services, write or call:

National Hospice Organization
1901 North Moore Street, Suite 901
Arlington, VA 22209
(1-800-658-8898)

5

The Cyanide Enigma

Is death by ingestion of cyanide the best means of self-deliverance? Is it as fast and as painless as it appears to be in the James Bond movies where the villain appears to die in twelve seconds? Is death by cyanide painful? Does it always work? Where can I get some? These questions come to me frequently from people planning for a quick and painless death.

Some of the most famous suicides in modern history have been by cyanide. Hermann Göring escaped the gallows at the Nuremburg trials in 1945 by biting on a glass vial of cyanide within a brass bullet that had been smuggled into his cell. Wallace Carothers, the inventor of nylon, who had a doctorate in organic chemistry, committed suicide in a hotel room in Philadelphia in 1937 by drinking potassium cyanide in lemon juice.

Perhaps the world's most unrecognized genius, Alan Turing, who developed the theory behind the computer in the 1930s and was a key player in cracking the German Enigma secret military codes, took his life in 1954 while under personal stress. Like Snow White, he bit into a poisoned apple dipped in "witches' brew." But, unlike the fairy tale, Turing had dipped his fruit in a jar of potassium cyanide solution and there could be no awakening by a prince's kiss.

About 800 of the 913 people who died in Jonestown, Guyana, in 1978 took potassium cyanide that had been put into a soft drink. The adults drank from cups; many of the children had it squirted down their throats by syringes.

In what I consider to be the most reliable of all accounts of the tragic mass suicide, San Francisco journalist Tim Reiterman, who was wounded in the shooting event that preceded the mass deaths and murders, reported that "parents and grandparents cried hysterically as their children died—not quickly and not painlessly. The doomed convulsed and gagged as the poison took effect. For several minutes they vomited, they screamed, they bled." (*Raven: The Untold Story of the Rev. Jim Jones and His People,* Dutton, New York, 1982.)

We do not know whether Göring, Turing, and Carothers suffered pain or not. That is the dilemma of death by cyanide—it is almost always a solitary act with no recovery. Remarkably few who take cyanide live to tell the tale, but the Jonestown massacre was so huge that some persons witnessed what went on.

Even in some well-planned suicides by cyanide, death is not always certain. In 1987 two terrorists, being questioned in Bahrain in connection with the bombing of a jet airliner, bit on cyanide contained within cigarettes. An eyewitness said: "Just after taking the cyanide, they both fell to the floor and their bodies went very stiff." The man died four hours later, but the woman terrorist recovered to stand trial.

During an arrest in connection with the murder of twenty-five people in northern California in 1985, a suspect bit on one of several cyanide pills in his possession. He died four days later in a hospital.

Clearly, experts feel it is the most effective method of self-destruction: more than 40 percent of the suicides among chemists, both men and women, occur from swallowing cyanide, according to a report in *The New York Times* (9/4/87).

This account was given to me by the son of a chemist in New Jersey: "After his retirement, when he was thinking about ending his life as his prostate cancer advanced, my father went to a chemical supply house and purchased a bottle of twelve ounces of ferrocyanide, and a few other related chemicals so as not to arouse suspicion. He was very forthright and open about this with his family. On the bottle of ferrocyanide he wrote, 'This is my control.' About six months later he dissolved a teaspoonful in half a glass of water and added a little vinegar to help release the cyanide gas, even though the natural acid in the stomach is probably sufficient. He died in my mother's arms after two breaths and no indication of pain or violence." But note, this man was a chemist.

A doctor tells me of a friend of his, a university professor, who prepared a cyanide capsule that he took with a glass of strong lemonade, and was found dead the next day sitting in his easy chair in a relaxed attitude.

A rare eyewitness account appeared in the London newspaper *Today* (9/16/87) in which a 27-year-old woman, severely crippled in a road accident, elected to end her life by sipping cyanide and water through a straw. A woman friend who was present took a photograph and made a recording of her wish to die. A peaceful death occurred thirteen seconds after the drink was consumed, according to the report.

Contrast this with the view of a doctor friend of mine who says he has had direct knowledge of a suicide by cyanide that was "miserable and violent, marked by frequent tetanic convulsions while awake. It was painful in the extreme. I would absolutely not recommend it."

Other doctors I have talked to about cyanide referred to the lack of medical knowledge on the subject. All had an impression that, although it was quick, it was also painful. They would only use it themselves as a very last resort.

Those states in America that have used gas chambers to judicially execute murderers give us some knowledge of the effect of hydrogen cyanide (HCN). Unconsciousness is supposed to be instant, with death following in five to ten minutes. But recently this method of execution has come into question as some evidence has emerged that death is neither quick nor painless. Increasingly, states use a massive infusion of drugs directly into the veins of the prisoner, who is strapped to a gurney. First, sodium thiopental is used to put the condemned individual to sleep; then follows Pavulon, a muscle relaxant similar to the South American poison curare, together with potassium chloride to stop the heart.

Reports indicate that consciousness is lost almost immediately and death follows within ten minutes. Doctors and nurses have always refused to participate in executions, and their professional organizations have supported them. This is understandable, but may have resulted in some bungled executions when an untrained person has not found the prisoner's vein properly and the needle slipped out.

In the Netherlands, where assisted suicide has been widely practiced for some twenty years with the consent of the courts and parliament, doctors will not even consider cyanide, even though a significant number of patients elect to drink a prescribed lethal drug themselves. Doctors have concocted other potions that they consider superior; this will be explained in a later chapter. Whether their dismissal stems from a prejudice against cyanide as an infamous chosen means of exit by depressed people, or from scientific judgment, is hard to assess. The world's leading expert on practical euthanasia, Dr. Pieter V. Admiraal, an anesthesiologist who lives in the Netherlands and is author of the booklet *Justifiable Euthanasia: A Guide to Physicians,* tells me: "I have no experience with cyanide. Rumor tells me that it's cruel to see . . . cramps and vomiting . . . with many minutes of awareness."

The textbooks tell us that hydrocyanic acid and its sodium and potassium salts are about the most potent and swift-acting poisons known to man. But they do not say whether their action is painless. There is cyanide present in many rodenticides and in the seeds of most common fruits, notably cherries, plums, and apricots. Cyanide comes in different forms: hydrocyanic acid, nitroprusside, potassium cyanide, and sodium cyanide. The compounds of cyanide have wide industrial applications: electroplating, ore-extracting processes, photography, polishing metals, and the fumigation of warehouses and ships. Death can come from inhalation of a mere 50 mg of the acid, while between 200 and 300 mg of the potassium or sodium salt is usually fatally toxic.

"If large amounts have been absorbed, collapse is usually instantaneous, the patient falling unconscious, often with a loud cry and dying almost immediately." (*Poisoning: Toxicology, Symptoms, Treatments,* by Jay M. Arena and Charles C. Thomas, Illinois.) Most of the textbooks speak of "convulsions, coma and death within five minutes." News reports and textbooks of suicides almost always speak of the strong smell of almonds and foam on the victim's mouth.

"If the stomach is empty and free, gastric acidity is high, poisoning is especially fast. After large doses, some victims have had time only for a warning cry before sudden loss of consciousness." (*Clinical Toxicology of Commercial Products. Acute Poisoning.* Gosselin, Hodge, Smith and Gleason, 4th edition. Williams and Wilkins, Baltimore and London.)

The Nazis murdered millions of Jews, Gypsies, homosexuals, political dissidents, and mentally and physically handicapped people in Germany between 1940 and 1945, mainly by the use of cyanide acid gas, which they called Zyklon B. These barbarous mass murders were swift, although, once again, we are unsure of the pain. The postwar Nuremburg trials meted out justice to the Nazi criminals. For their part in the so-called "mercy euthanasia" of the handicapped, four doctors were hanged at Nuremburg and five others sentenced to life imprisonment. Others were caught and tried later. It was a failure by a section of the medical profession to discipline itself ethically, and it must never be allowed to happen again.

I believe that the balance of evidence about using cyanide indicates it is best not used. Also, it is difficult to obtain unless a person knows the trade outlets and has the credentials to make a purchase. But if a person possesses cyanide and is determined to use it to escape the ravages of terminal illness, this is the technique:

1. Take a small glass of cold tap water.
2. Stir one gram, or 1.5 gm at most, of KCN (potassium cyanide) into the water. (Larger amounts would cause burning of the throat.)
3. After about five minutes, the KCN is dissolved and ready to drink. It remains drinkable for several hours, but not more.
4. Once the potion is drunk, consciousness will be lost in about a minute. There will be just time to rinse out the glass so that nobody else accidentally drinks from it, and then lie down. But beware: a person extremely

weakened by illness might black out in twenty seconds.

5. While in the coma, death will follow in fifteen minutes, or at most forty-five minutes, depending on the
physical strength of the person and whether the stomach is full or empty. An empty stomach (with cyanide) promotes faster death.

6. During the coma period, the dying person will breathe
heavily and snore loudly, similar to people who have
taken an overdose of barbiturates.

The key to the effectiveness of cyanide as a killer is the
water. This is borne out by evidence in textbooks that flocks
of sheep that have eaten plants containing cyanide do not
die so long as they do not drink. If the animals are near
water, the plants are fatal.

Because no caring persons would want loved ones or
friends to witness what might be a painful death, I remain
skeptical about self-deliverance using any form of cyanide.
There are better ways, as I shall explain.

6

Death Hollywood Style

People often ask me whether there are ways of achieving a graceful and pain-free self-deliverance by some method other than drugs or a plastic bag. They have seen movies in which people took their lives in a quick and easy way, or read detective stories where a character found a rare poison that did the job and no one could tell.

Death by self-injection of air into a vein is the most common procedure inquired about. The aesthetic attractiveness of this antiseptic method of accelerated death—apparently clean, bloodless, clinical, swift, and painless—obviously fascinates many people. Writers of crime mystery stories—first and most notably Dorothy L. Sayers—have glamorized it ever since that literary genre first flourished in the 1920s.

Whenever a Hollywood movie script calls for a suicide, the air bubble method is favored by directors. In *Coming Home,* for instance, the 1978 film about disillusioned veterans returning from the Vietnam War, starring Jane Fonda and Jon Voight, a man is fleetingly seen committing suicide by injection of air from a syringe. A segment of the television hospital drama series *St. Elsewhere* has a male character killing himself by the same method. A woman wrote to me: "It looked so nice and easy. Is it really?"

A review of the available medical literature shows only one case of it actually happening, and that instance has ambiguous features. In 1949 Dr. Herman Sander, a New Hampshire general practitioner, injected 40 cc's of air into the veins of a cancer patient, Mrs. Abbie Burotto, aged fifty-nine. She was in the final terminal stages of her illness. Unwisely, Dr. Sander entered into the hospital records the statement: "Patient given ten cc's of air intravenously, repeated three times. Expired ten minutes after this was started."

A person at the hospital who maintained the records saw this unusual entry and reported it to her superiors. Dr. Sander was immediately arrested.

The case became a *cause célèbre* in euthanasia and aroused enormous public attention at the time, much of it in support of Dr. Sander. At his trial in 1950, Dr. Sander pleaded not guilty to first-degree murder and denied that his injection of air caused the patient's death. One physician testified that he could find no pulse during an examination on the morning of Mrs. Burotto's death, and that she might have expired before Dr. Sander gave the injection. A nurse also said that she thought the woman was dead before both doctors saw her.

Although found not guilty of the crime, Dr. Sander had his license to practice medicine revoked. There was a public outcry and it was later reinstated. It was reported that his medical practice increased considerably.

Does it work? Is this a practical form of euthanasia for either the patient or a doctor to use?

First, it is probably detectable in an autopsy, because air bubbles would most likely gather in the right side of the heart. It is assumed by doctors who have given the matter some thought that, while some bubbles may get through to the lungs, the air embolus in the heart itself prevents anything from going to the lungs.

A professor of anatomy told me: "What it feels like is, of course, impossible to say, because I don't imagine anyone has survived the injection of enough air to fill the heart chambers. Small quantities of air would pass through and out to the lungs, and would produce a shutdown of activity in small segments of the lung, probably without much sensation."

Dr. Colin Brewer, a London physician and psychiatrist who has studied all forms of euthanasia for a quarter of a century, commented: "As far as I can recall from my medical teaching, air embolism certainly causes a rapid death, though whether it is a particularly pleasant one I simply don't know. And since it is exceedingly rare I don't suppose many other people know either. You certainly would have to inject quite a bit of air very quickly, otherwise it is absorbed before the blood has reached the heart. Nurses are usually fanatical about removing the last, tiny bubble from anything they inject, but I understand that you need to inject at least twenty cc's, which is an awful lot of bubbles. The air has to be injected into a vein, and I imagine a lot of people will not find this easy to do themselves, especially if they are elderly, since old people's veins tend to be tricky to get into." (Private communication to the author.)

Professor Yvon Kenis, a veteran oncologist who is also head of a Belgian euthanasia society, tells me that in his long career he has never come across any instance of death by this method, although he was told about the risks in medical school.

"My impression is that this is not a suitable method, nor a gentle death in humans," Professor Kenis said. "Particularly, it would be extremely difficult to utilize as a method of suicide. During the injection, the first part of the air may induce temporary cardiac arrest and loss of consciousness. This might be reversible, possibly with very serious consequences, such as paralysis or permanent brain damage. I have to stress that this is only an impression and that I have no real scientific information on the subject."

Dr. Pieter Admiraal describes the theoretical air bubble method of suicide as impossible, disagreeable, and cruel. "To kill somebody with air you have to inject at least 100 to 200 ml as quickly as possible in a vein as big as possible close to the heart. You would have to fill the whole heart with air at once. The heart would probably beat on for several minutes, perhaps five to fifteen minutes, and during the first minutes the person may be conscious."

The moral of all these comments from medical experts is that one should definitely not imitate the stories found in books and movies.

7

Bizarre Ways to Die

This chapter is really unnecessary for the serious reader. But I have to include it because people write to me constantly with ideas for self-destruction about which they have heard, or invented themselves, that they believe will achieve a quick and peaceful death. A good deal of my time is spent writing back saying, "No, I don't think so. Not recommended."

A significant section of the public is fascinated by curious and outlandish ways to kill oneself. So I will deal with bizarre suicides here—if I don't, my mail from people who feel cheated will increase significantly—and then we can get back to serious considerations.

First, let me relate some truly weird cases of suicidal techniques.

As the sun rose one day in Seattle in 1986, it triggered a device that shot its inventor. This man, a disturbed and unhappy electronics engineer, had set up a photoelectric cell in the window of his motel room. A wire from the cell ran to a device with elements that he placed on his chest. Sunlight heated the elements, which in turn detonated a firecracker. The explosion of the firecracker released a firing pin from a gun, which shot a round straight into his heart. I suppose, for a man with his interests, it was "going out in appropriate style," but it is way beyond the capabilities of most of us.

Another depressed man in southern California who collected rattlesnakes as a hobby deliberately allowed one of his pets to bite him five or six times on the right hand. He suffered a fatal heart attack.

For sheer determination, this 1987 story is hard to top. A 22-year-old man in England, who broke up with his girlfriend, threw himself at four different cars and a truck, tried to strangle himself, and jumped out of a window. He lived to tell the tale, as they say, for all he needed was hospital treatment for minor injuries!

A 23-year-old man in Austria who was suffering from AIDS killed himself by deliberately driving his car into an oncoming railway train. Driving cars into barriers, abutments, or trees is a frequent method of suicide, undoubtedly made attractive by the hope that it will not be considered a suicide. But with the wearing of safety belts in vehicles today now mandatory in so many places, not wearing one in a one-vehicle crash arouses suspicion of suicide.

Recently I read about the death of an 85-year-old man

who died when making his first parachute jump. His chute did not open and it was ruled an accident. Given the man's age, I wonder if it was a form of aerial euthanasia. Some people do choose bizarre means of killing themselves. We shall never know in this case.

Government statistics show that just about 31,000 people in the United States commit suicide every year—by no means the world's highest rate—but experts who have studied suicidal behavior say that the true rate is certainly double, and perhaps triple, that number because so many go undetected or unreported.

The drawbacks to many forms of suicide need to be made clear to people, because it is a subject surrounded by legend and myth.

ELECTROCUTION. Workmen are sometimes killed by electric shock, but some have miraculous survivals. Sometimes survival from a shock results in serious paralysis and bodily harm. Nowadays most electrical systems are so heavily protected with fuses and cut-out devices that they will short-circuit and cease to transmit current under strain. Some people tell me that their mode of self-deliverance will be getting into the bathtub and pulling an electric heater in after them. It might work, and it might not. The worst danger is that the person finding the body might rush to help and also be electrocuted. Unless a person is an ingenious electrical engineer, electricity is definitely not advised for self-deliverance.

HANGING. Self-destruction by hanging is almost always an act of protest, a desire to shock and hurt someone. Therefore, believers in euthanasia avoid it. Even if the job of cutting down the body is left to the police or paramedics, this is an unacceptably selfish way to die, and I have never heard of a euthanasia supporter using it. Unless the neck is broken by the rope jerking the fall to a stop (as a professional hangman arranges), then it is death by strangulation, often not so quick.

DROWNING. Death comes quickly in bitterly cold water from hypothermia. The lower the temperature, the faster the end. But there is always the chance that someone of whom you are not aware is watching and there is a possibility of rescue. This manner of suicide also leaves unanswered questions for survivors. Was it deliberate (if no note is left) or accidental? Will the body ever be found? Will there be an extensive search for the body, risking other people's lives and a great deal of public expense?

SHOOTING. This is definitely not the final exit of choice for believers in euthanasia, because you cannot have somebody else present at death. Moreover, it is bloody and violent, and who has the awful task of cleaning up? A properly aimed gun is preferred by many because of its speed and painlessness, but it is not unknown for people to shoot themselves and miss. A slight deviation of the gun barrel and the bullet misses vital organs but inflicts terrible wounds. Reports in newspapers and journals indicate that the preferred method is to put the gun into the mouth and shoot upward, but even here there have sometimes been survivors.

Some of the best-planned shootings go wrong. In 1945 as American occupation troops approached his home in Tokyo, General Tojo, Japan's prime minister, prepared to kill himself. He had his doctor make a chalk mark on his chest in the area of his heart; then, when the troops were at the front door, he fired a .32 Colt into the spot. Although seriously wounded, he missed the heart and lived to be tried for war crimes. Tojo was hanged three years later.

The bigger the gun, the more likely it is to be effective; and a hollow-point bullet makes a larger wound. A .22-caliber gun is not always lethal, and determined individuals often have to fire twice. To use a gun for self-destruction is to invite a judgment of suicide in the worst sense of the word. Terminally ill and irreversibly ill people who want accelerated death to avoid further suffering resort to more gentle and less shocking methods.

OVENS. In the first half of this century, putting the head in a gas oven was a common method of suicide. But this is not possible today because of the use of "natural gas" pumped from the earth, which is not lethal like the old "city gas" made in retorts.

CHARCOAL COOKING FIRES. There have been many sad cases of accidental deaths of people who lit charcoal fires in tents or rooms without proper ventilation. But this method done deliberately for suicide carries with it a huge potential for explosion or fires that could kill other people. Sometimes the gas has leaked into the rooms where innocent people were sleeping. In Florida in 1996 a French woman on vacation decided to kill herself by gas; not only did she die, but also her husband and daughter, which she had not intended—her suicide note spoke of her wanting them to live without her being a burden. Additionally, if a person is discovered alive after serious inhalation of these gases, the chance of mental and physical impairment is high.

Household cleaning and drain-clearance chemicals. The means of death certainly lies under almost every household kitchen sink. Bleach, lye, and drain-cleaning fluids will kill if taken in quantity. The manner of death is painful in the extreme as the throat and/or stomach is burned out by the acid. I have heard of people throwing themselves through plate-glass windows in their death agonies after drinking lye.

Poisonous plants. Many people are obsessed with the thought that they can pluck a plant or a shrub from their garden and bring about their own demise in a natural fashion. My mailbag is full of such inquiries. Yes, the water plant hemlock, foxglove, oleander, and some other plants can be toxic to the point of lethality. But how much is lethal? No one really knows, since it depends on the age of the plant, the time of the year, the condition of the person, the content of the stomach, and so forth. What might kill a child—the most frequent victim of accidental poisoning—might not kill an adult. Everything I have ever read about death from plant poisoning indicates that it is risky and very painful. Symptoms range from nausea and vomiting to cramping and bloody diarrhea. Burned mouths, dizziness, and visual disturbances are other side effects. Reporting on cases of geriatric patients who had deliberately eaten oleander leaves, the *Western Journal of Medicine* (12/89) said patients either died or survived through differences in age, health of organ system, oleander species, and poison preparation. Moreover, while identification and naming has been a science since the Middle Ages, the toxicity of plants is far from being an exact science. Too much depends on the site of growth and the time of year the plant is picked. Altogether, I consider poisonous plants as a means of exit far too unreliable and painful. No matter how desperately ill you are, don't even think about plants.

Freezing. Not so bizarre, and a method for which I have respect, is freezing to death on a mountain. It takes a certain sort of person to want to die this way: having a love of and knowledge of mountains, determination, and the enduring courage to carry it off. Of course, the person must be strong enough to make the journey upward. A few terminally ill persons I have known have quietly ascended their favorite mountain late in the day and made sure that they were above the freezing line for that particular time of the year. They used public transport to get there so that a parked car would not be spotted. Then, wearing light clothing, they sat down in a secluded spot to await the end. Some have said that they intended to take a tranquilizer or sleeping pill to hasten the sleep of death. From what we know of hypothermia they would pass out anyway as the cold dropped to a certain level, and they would die within hours. Of course, in a very cold climate there is no need to climb a mountain.

The originators of this way of death were the Eskimos, who used ice floes, and the Japanese, who climbed mountains. In Japanese lore, if the person was unfit to climb the mountain, a son had to carry his parent on his back. Remember, though, that the Eskimos practiced this form of euthanasia as a form of group survival so that the tribe could move fast enough across the tundra to hunt for food needed for survival. The Japanese did it out of poverty. I do not think this same practice occurs with these two groups today, but a few modern believers in euthanasia have adopted the practice as their preferred method of exit.

When choosing to die on a mountain or similar lonely place, it is considerate to leave a note saying where your body can be found. Otherwise, people might risk their lives and expend considerable resources hunting in dangerous places for you.

NONPRESCRIPTION DRUGS. Because people are frustrated at not being able to secure barbiturate drugs from their doctor, hardly a day goes by without a letter in my mail asking if such and such an over-the-counter drug is lethal.

Certainly it is possible to commit suicide with huge amounts of some drugs bought at a pharmacy without a prescription, but the dying will be slow and painful—and perhaps fail. For example, extremely heavy doses of aspirin will burn the lining of the stomach over several days. These "weak" drugs, even if lethal, will take so long—perhaps days—to end a life that somebody is bound to discover what is happening and put you in a hospital, where your stomach will be pumped out or antidotes administered. There is also the possibility of permanent brain or physical damage with a botched attempt.

Many drugs are lethal if taken in great overdose, but the dying will be slow and painful, and a resuscitation, which you don't want when terminally ill, is probable. The only nonprescription drugs that can be effectively utilized are sleep aids in combination with a plastic bag, which we will discuss later.

8

The Dilemma of the Severely Handicapped

Not many people who are paraplegics or quadriplegics wish to kill themselves. But some do. Either they are unable to bear their grave disability, or, more likely, they are terminally ill. Most severely handicapped people bear their affliction with great courage and resourcefulness and make useful lives.

There is no more controversial aspect of euthanasia than that involving the handicapped. Merely to mention it causes my critics to call me "murderer" and "Nazi" and claim I want to get rid of the "burdens on society." Not so. Severely handicapped people have an inalienable right either to live or choose to die just the same as anybody else. I respect the right of that small number of handicapped persons who want—either now or in the future—to have available the option of self-deliverance or doctor-assisted suicide without being preached to, and patronized by, those on the religious right.

James Haig was a young man whose will to live had died in a terrible road accident although his shattered body lived on. I was attending a world euthanasia conference in Oxford, England, in 1980 when James came in a wheelchair and asked to talk to me privately. He had been thrown from his motorcycle after colliding with a car and was left, at age 24, permanently paralyzed from the neck down. Restricted use of his right fingers allowed him to operate an electric wheelchair. James had struggled for four years to cope with the shock of being changed from an active sportsman and husband and father into an eighty-four-pound quadriplegic. He had been cared for in the best hospitals in England and received extensive psychological counseling to try to help him come to grips with this disaster. Accident insurance had provided ample money for him to live on, an excellent, specially adapted home, and transportation facilities.

But James could not accept his condition. He divorced his wife against her wishes. He then joined the Voluntary Euthanasia Society, in London, but found that while that organization was sympathetic it could not directly help him. James twice tried to arrange his own self-destruction. First he drove his wheelchair into the Thames River, but it was low tide, the wheels stuck in the mud, and he was ignominiously dragged out. A second time, he arranged with a friend to provide drugs in a motel room, but the friend changed his mind at the last moment and reneged. James Haig's case became so notorious—and moving—that it was reported extensively in the British newspapers, which did his cause no good because now whoever helped him die would reap a blaze of publicity.

At his Oxford meeting with me, James explained his personal philosophy. Despite all the care, love, and money that had been lavished on him, he said he simply could not continue to live in this smashed condition. He wished to end it. "Help me to die, Derek," he pleaded. I demurred. "But you helped Jean to die. Then why not me?"

I had narrowly escaped prosecution in 1978 for helping my terminally ill wife to die (recounted in the book *Jean's Way*) and had only just set up the Hemlock Society in America to fight for lawful assistance in dying. Additionally, my personal philosophy is that I am willing to break the law forbidding assistance in suicide, if I have to, for a loved one or dear friend, but not for a stranger, which James was.

Secondly, I had just launched a highly visible, long-range campaign to educate people in the hope that the law would be reformed to permit voluntary physician-assisted dying in justifiable cases. Therefore, to engage in another assistance—to a stranger—would both have clashed with my ethics and be counterproductive to my reform efforts. I urged him to find a person close to him who would help. He was deeply disappointed, but I felt he understood and we parted on good terms.

A few months later I read in the newspapers than James had indeed committed suicide—by setting his house on fire and allowing himself to burn to death. Somehow he had managed to set an armchair on fire and park his wheelchair next to it. He left a suicide note. I—and probably the numerous other people whom James asked for help—have been troubled by the manner of his death and wondered if we should have helped provide a more dignified and painless way.

The moral and legal difficulties of the question of voluntary assisted dying for the severely handicapped was never more clearly delineated than by the story of Elizabeth Bouvia. Paralyzed since birth by cerebral palsy, in 1983 she decided that her existence was not worth continuing and checked herself into a California hospital, asking to be allowed to starve herself to death.

The hospital refused cooperation and went to court seeking permission to force-feed Elizabeth. (She lost the first case but won the second: you cannot be force-fed in California.) A television clip of the court proceedings showed her asking with great determination and intelligence to be allowed to die by starvation. The case developed into an international media circus, and Elizabeth got all the attention she had obviously been craving. There was talk of a book and a movie about her life. I followed the proceedings at a distance because I also noticed the evidence of considerable recent unhappiness in Elizabeth's life—including a failed marriage and a miscarriage. Might that not be the force driving her to suicide?

Anyway, after all the court battles proved that she had the right to starve herself to death if she wished but could not demand that anyone help her, she changed her mind. She was still alive and well cared for in a Los Angeles hospital twelve years later.

In 1992, a young man came to see me at a conference in Long Beach, California, asking for advice on his suicide. He was in a wheelchair because a bullet fired at him by a "freeway bandit" had smashed his spine as he was driving his car several years earlier. He was a healthy-looking man in his twenties, and his upper torso worked well. With him were loving parents. He told me he had been in contact with Dr. Jack Kevorkian, the retired Michigan pathologist who sometimes helps people to die, but he was uncertain about whether to travel to Michigan. As we talked over the situation it became clear that continual physical pain was the main problem driving him to think of self-destruction. By then another doctor also at the conference had joined in the conversation and quickly detected a medical mistake in the young man's medications, and over the next few weeks radically changed them to relieve the pain and discomfort. This young man, like Elizabeth Bouvia, lives on.

For every case I could cite of severely handicapped people changing their minds on suicide, I could cite another where they did not, and went through with their self-deliverance because the suffering and indignity was unbearable to them. The handicapped become terminally ill like the rest of us, often earlier because of underlying health problems caused by inactivity. For twenty years I have met handicapped people in wheelchairs who come to my public meetings around the world and—to summarize their views—tell me that they want the option of euthanasia as an insurance against the physical deterioration and sapping illnesses that so often come from enforced inactivity. Some whom I knew in the 1980s are now dead by their own hand; others are still enjoying life.

The terrible dilemma of the quadriplegic is—as James Haig's story so poignantly illustrates—how to end one's life when alone and helpless. It is nearly impossible to carry it out. Only in rare cases is some family member or friend willing to help. My files contain heartrending stories of loved ones suffocating, shooting, cutting the throats of, and supplying lethal drugs to handicapped people who desire death. Court proceedings, publicity, and sometimes imprisonment often follow. Sometimes people have the technical skill and determination to surmount the obstacles. In 1994 a disabled man in Chichester, England, who was paralyzed from the chest down after a fall, managed to kill himself by wiring his body to an electronic clock and setting the time of his death by electrocution for 3 A.M. Presumably everybody else was asleep at this hour, even he himself, but we do not know. His brother said at the inquest that this 35-year-old man had been in pain for years and had often spoken of euthanasia.

This letter from a woman to me describes the problem far better than I can:

"Three years ago I was in a car accident which left me paralyzed from the shoulders down. Though I had a Living Will, I did not have it present at the scene of the accident. I woke up in the Intensive Care Unit on a respirator at a trauma center, with a broken neck, punctured lungs, and a room full of monitors. By the time I became aware of my condition, there was no way that I could request to be taken off the respirator.

"My mind is extremely sharp and I am fully aware, but my quality of life has been reduced to mere existence. I can do nothing for myself. There is nothing I would like more than to be able to find someone to assist me in self-deliverance because I will never be happy with this lack of quality of life. However, it is impossible to find the type of assistance without some legislation or a friend in the medical field unafraid of the legal ramifications.

"I feel so trapped and utterly hopeless in this situation and have nowhere to turn. Life has no dignity and I feel as though I am sitting here waiting to die. . . . A life without quality and dignity is every bit as bad, if not worse, than terminal illness, where at least one knows that the misery will end, whereas my life may go on for many, many years."

What can those of us who sympathize with a justified suicide wish by a handicapped person do to help? As the legal and moral climate now stands in Western society, assistance is particularly dangerous. If it has to be undertaken, it should only be between people who are very close to each other and fully understand the situation. When we eventually have laws on the statute books that permit physician-assisted dying for the terminally ill, I believe that along with this reform will develop a more merciful and tolerant response to the type of rare cases that I have been describing in this chapter. These are so few that they do not justify special legislation—"hard cases make poor law," as the saying goes.

If a severely handicapped person and a helper feel they must proceed with euthanasia, the matter having been carefully considered and there being no acceptable alternative, then exceptional care must be taken regarding methods, privacy for the act, and subsequent secrecy. There is another old saying, "Necessity hath no law," but the police don't recognize that maxim. At the very least, friends of a handicapped person must function as a reasonable sounding board for the discussion of the pros and cons of the decision, and should carefully consider whether to give moral support.

I have monitored these type of cases for twenty years, and my conclusion is that close relatives get greater mercy from the courts than do friends. I suppose it is the old feeling of blood bonds and kinship influencing the jury and judges. Several years after it was decided I would not be prosecuted for assisting the suicide of my terminally ill wife, Jean, I met in London one of the detectives who had investigated my case. "Why did you not press for charges to be brought?" I asked him. He was reluctant to answer, but after a pause he said: "In this world you have to do what you have to do." And he turned away. Help from family members is preferable, of course, but sometimes there is only a friend who is available or will help.

9

Self-Starvation

Some people feel that starving themselves to death is the ideal euthanasia. There are numerous reports of extremely old people dying this way, and there is no reason to doubt them. But it is not as quick and simple as it sounds. There are many factors to consider.

Medical studies that detail the effects of death by starvation are remarkably few. It does not seem to be a subject with which doctors wish to get involved. There are some studies that report the effects of fasting as acts of protest. Most of these, thankfully, ended in a decision to cease the campaign and live.

These reports tell us that after approximately 20 percent of body-weight loss, illness of one sort or another begins to set in, notably severe indigestion, muscle weakness, and—

worst of all—mental incapacity. The health of a particular individual determines which illness comes first. A fit human in his or her forties can fast about forty days before life is seriously threatened. After that, there is a high risk of death. Exactly when this will occur will vary from person to person.

In some cases self-starvation can be very painful. In 1987, after a court in Colorado gave Hector Rodas permission to starve himself to death (he was a quadriplegic), morphine had to be administered to kill the pain of fatal dehydration. In the fifteen days it took Rodas, who had good medical care, to die he constantly slipped in and out of a coma. I believe it would have been more compassionate, once the court had given the green light for him to end his life, to have administered a fatal overdose. But the law did not—and still does not—permit this.

Physicians assure us that starvation of a patient in a persistent vegetative state (brain damaged beyond recovery) causes no suffering as long as there is good nursing care, which would include moistening of the lips. Such a person usually dies in ten to fourteen days. Of course, most such patients have been unconscious and bedridden for several years and have already deteriorated physically.

The medical profession made a great deal out of the death by starvation in 1994 of Virginia Eddy at the age of 85 in Middlebury, Vermont. She suffered from serious health problems associated with age. Doctors publicized her suicide as an ideal way to die, better than any form of euthanasia. Mrs. Eddy was quoted in a note to her son as saying: "Tell others about how well this worked for me. I'd like this to be my gift. Whether they are terminally ill, in intractable pain, or, like me, just know that the right time has come for them, more people might want to know that this way exists. And perhaps more physicians will help them find it."

Mrs. Eddy died within a week of deciding to forgo all food and fluids. It was, apparently, a peaceful and dignified death, which the old lady deserved. But could we all expect such a beneficent end? Consider the facts: Her son was David M. Eddy, a professor of health policy and management at Duke University and a senior adviser to Kaiser Permanente, southern California. He supervised his mother's end, ensuring that she had enough morphine patches to control the pain of starvation. Doctors listen to doctors, especially one of Dr. Eddy's eminence, and this was Mrs. Eddy's good fortune.

Without a close relative who is a physician, most patients in poor quality-of-life situations like Mrs. Eddy's are unable to get assistance in dying. Instead the leaders of the medical profession continue to resist all attempts, educational and legal, to legitimize aid-in-dying unless it involves one of their own. Dr. Eddy's article describing at length his mother's "gentle death" appeared in the prestigious *Journal of the American Medical Association* and was widely repeated in the lay press. I am glad Mrs. Eddy died the way she wanted, but it was undeniably an example of elitism. It also again illustrated the medical fact that starvation for a conscious person can be painful, because she needed morphine.

Another famous death by self-starvation, which is sometimes called "silent suicide," was that of social pioneer and writer Scott Nearing, in Cape Rosier, Maine, in 1983. Scott's death is often referred to as an ideal way to die quickly and painlessly. He got the death he wanted, but, again, the facts bear examination as they are related by his widow, Helen, in her book *Loving and Leaving the Good Life*.

As Scott approached his 100th birthday he announced one day: "I think I won't eat anymore." This was a man of great inner strengths and iron self-discipline, which not all of us possess, and, with the loving cooperation of his wife, who understood his reasoning that his life was over, he took no more food. Two facts that are in the book but are usually ignored in reports of Scott's manner of death are that he took liquids for the remainder of his life, and—probably because there was no dehydration—he took six weeks to die. As I commented with respect to Mrs. Eddy, it was the type of death that Scott Nearing wanted, and through his courage and with a loving, caring wife, received. But before you think about the same final exit, consider carefully your own situation.

A Chicago woman of my acquaintance who was 88, suffering from what I call "terminal old age" after a mild stroke and congestive heart failure, still took thirty-three days to die from self-starvation. Even though she had considered the decision very carefully and was determined to die, that did not speed things up. She also stopped taking all her heart medications. She took half a cup of water each day and moistened her lips with ice cubes. Three days before her death she began having mild hallucinations and her doctor treated her with Thorazine. After that she slept constantly and died peacefully at her daughter's home.

Her daughter told me: "Needless to say, it was painful to watch her deterioration. I was surprised that she survived so long, because I thought that once she made up her mind she would quickly die—partly because we stopped the digoxin but significantly because she was so strong-willed. I finally suggested to her that fighting to die might be life-asserting. She then relaxed more and repeated: 'I am at peace.' As the days passed she often stated that she felt very lucky to be experiencing feelings of love and goodwill to all."

Self-starvation has a distinct appeal for some. It is essentially an independent action, taking responsibility for your own death, involving no others in possibly illegal actions. It is demonstrating a desire to die at this point because of an unacceptable quality of life. But the possibility of further illness before death comes, and the effect of that on loved ones, plus the uncertain length of the process, must be carefully considered.

Remember, there are two ways to starve oneself to death: without food and fluids, which is the quicker way but more painful; and with fluids only, which is slower but less painful. In both methods, painkilling drugs are desirable.

Force-feeding is not permitted in Western society. Numerous court cases have underlined that no medical treatment can be administered without the patient's consent, even in life-threatening situations.

10

The Will to Die and "Miracle Cures"

An aunt of mine died recently in her eighties from a perforated bowel. She also had numerous other illnesses that, singly or in combination, would eventually have killed her. It was a matter of which illness got her first. She longed to die. "I pray to God to take me now," she would say. But she lingered for months and suffered physically and mentally. She was so debilitated by her illnesses that life gave her no pleasure. While she recognized my work in the field of euthanasia, and spoke approvingly of it, her religious beliefs would not permit her to accelerate the end in any way. I respected that.

A willingness to die is insufficient alone to bring about death. It would be nice if that were all that were necessary. I have heard direct accounts of people who were terribly sick with one or two terminal illnesses who made planned and determined attempts at suicide, hovered on the brink of death, and failed because of insufficient lethal dosages or a drug interaction that neutralized the lethal effects. In these cases I am convinced that if it were possible to will oneself to death, some would have succeeded because they were so close to death anyway.

Some people think differently about this. They have confidently told me that all they will need to do when they are terminal and close to the end is to get into the right frame of mind and within a day or so will stop breathing. I think an Indian Yogi who has devoted long years to the control of mind over the body might be able to achieve that type of death, but not the average person. Some doctors who specialize in the care of geriatric patients have told me that there are rare occasions when they have heard a very old, sick, and frail person announce, "I'm going to die today." And the individual did. But it doesn't happen often.

In the 1990 movie *Longtime Companion,* there is an emotional scene where a young gay man suffering from advanced AIDS dies. Film critic David Jansen, in his review in *Newsweek,* writes of the dying man's gay lover "helping him to die." But after watching the movie myself, I think the help referred to is more accurately described as "giving permission to die." Over and over, at the sick man's bedside, the companion urges, "Let go. It's all right to let go. Let go." And the sick man stops fighting for life and dies. Again, we are dealing with fiction, of course, and we are not told exactly how long the dying process took or how close the patient was to death when the "permission" was given.

Beware of taking ideas about death and dying from books and films. The accounts have almost always been sanitized, and certainly, to maintain viewers' interest, the time span has been much abbreviated. Sometimes (as mentioned earlier) the accounts are extremely misleading.

Having stated my skepticism, however, I do believe that a well-thought-out willingness to die, accepting that one's life has run its full course, and also having express permission from the loved ones to depart, does help—if only a bit. It frees the patient from familial and social obligations to stay alive and fight on when the battle is hopeless. In certain cases death might be precipitated by not taking any more medications, but stopping drug therapy to bring about death is risky and may cause suffering. Of course, if the patient is connected to life-support equipment and elects to have it taken off, that settles the matter.

Summing up, it is my view that the will to die in euthanasia is preferable and helps the process but should not be relied upon as the definitive release mechanism.

"Miracle Cures"

On the other side of the coin, a lot of people wonder about the possibility of a "miracle cure" being announced the day after they have deliberately ended their life. It is the most natural thing in the world, when we have a serious disease, to hope that the long-awaited scientific breakthrough is going to happen here and now to save us.

Medical science has made tremendous advances in this century and particularly in the past thirty years. Research and technology march forward on many promising fronts. The fact remains, however, that many types of cancer are not curable, though some are. Early detection and sophisticated treatment save many lives and usefully prolong others. There is, for instance, currently no cure for Alzheimer's disease, lupus, or Lou Gehrig's disease (amyotrophic lateral sclerosis, ALS).

My observation of the trends in modern medical science leads me to believe that the eventual answer to most of these diseases will come from *preventative* measures against illnesses to which we are prone, probably traced through genetics, rather than the cure of an illness that has already taken hold.

I cannot find any evidence of sudden miracle cures in medical history. Penicillin, for instance, was discovered by Alexander Fleming in the mid-1930s but did not come onto the market until the second half of the next decade, and has since saved many lives. Enormous progress has been made in combating leukemia in children, but the medical literature shows that it was a battle fought over at least a decade. At one stage the drug interferon was internationally hailed as the answer to most cancers; with further testing it proved to be of small help.

In the event of a complete cure for a disease being suddenly found, it is unlikely to help a patient who has already been seriously damaged by the ravages of the disease. Vital organs or important tissue may have been destroyed, which is what is bringing the patient to the brink of death and stimulating the desire to have control over the event. Additionally, many drug treatments—notably intensive chemotherapy—cause damage to the body while at the same time fighting off the disease. Thus a "miracle cure," regardless of how miraculous it is, would, if it happened, undoubtedly be more effective at the beginning of an illness than in the final stages.

Definitely ask your physician about promising research in the illness for which you are being treated. Hunt out yourself the latest medical literature on the subject. Study the papers closely and see if there seems to be a relevance to your illness. If there is, take the documents to your treating physician or specialist and talk them over.

Watch the medical sections of the weekly newsmagazines and newspapers. Progress in medicine is something upbeat that the media loves to report. Take anything you learn back to your physician for joint evaluation.

Progress in medicine comes only after years of dogged research and testing, then followed by an elaborate evaluation by a government agency—usually in America the Food and Drug Administration—with the purpose of assuring that the procedure does what its finders claim for it, and that there are no harmful side effects.

There is another aspect of "miracle cures"—the belief that they could be brought about by a deity. Deeply religious people may believe in waiting for a medical miracle brought about by divine intervention, and that is their right. (Such persons would be unlikely to be reading this book.)

And yet, with all the medical advances in the world,

death will eventually come to us all. It is up to the judgment of each individual to determine when medical treatment should be discontinued, and if it is the time to bring life to an end.

11

Who Shall Know?

Whom do you want to know about your death, and do you want them also to know that you chose to bring your own life to a close? The answer to the first part of the question is personal to you, of course, but I do recommend that you are frank about the second. Nothing is worse than ill-informed gossip and, once you are gone, there is no chance for you to set the record straight; thus, your true reason for speeding up the end may go unnoticed.

It is imperative that your loved ones and close friends know in advance what you are contemplating. Do not surprise or shock them with a *fait accompli*. Casually informing them that you are a member of a right-to-die organization, or have just read this book, are opening gambits that can lead to a thoughtful conversation allowing you to explain your motives. If there is no reaction the first time from somebody who is important to you, mention it again later. They may have been surprised the first time but since had time to consider it carefully. Do this while you are healthy, if possible, or certainly early in a terminal illness. Don't leave raising the subject until it is too late.

There may be more support within your family than you realize. Many people are reluctant to discuss their private views on euthanasia in case they meet with shock and rebuttal. One woman I know was keeping it a tight family secret that she was planning to help her mother die, which she eventually did. After the funeral, she discovered that her aunt (her mother's sister) was a longtime member of her local right-to-die group. "It would have been so useful to have had Auntie's support," she told me. "I never dreamed that she was on that wavelength."

Additionally, be sure to tell your closest friends about your intentions. They might be hurt that you left without telling them and not saying good-bye. In her final months, my first wife, Jean, would drop into conversations with her girlfriends when her cancer was being discussed little phrases like: "I'm not going to the end, you know. I shall do something about it." One of the friends vividly remembered these hints, and when I was under investigation in 1978 for assisted suicide she told the police this. I believe it helped me by demonstrating whose scheme it was, for— although it must have been a close judgment call by the public prosecutor—I was not subsequently charged with any offense.

It all depends on your circumstances in life, of course,

but an alternative that many have used is to circulate a letter to your best friends setting out your intentions and your reasons. Doris Portwood, author of the groundbreaking book *Commonsense Suicide* in 1978, when the Parkinson's disease from which she suffered took a severe turn, ended her life at the beginning of 1996 with sixty Seconal and a slug of whiskey. Now unable to write by hand, she had a letter typed and copied to all her friends that started "This is a self-evident suicide note . . ." and ended "At 82 I have a progressively downhill disease. I must opt for a decision before my mental capabilities are further eroded."

Will it get into the newspapers? Whether the media wishes to report your death in the first place depends very much on who you are. The cause of death does not have to be given, although it is preferable and customary to do so, but if you don't want suicide mentioned give the underlying cause of the death instead—for instance, cancer or heart disease. Nowadays it is frequently reported within obituaries of both major and minor public figures that the person took his or her own life toward the end of a terminal disease. It is no longer a shameful thing to say. The act of speeding up the end is not mentioned in the headlines.

Occasionally I see death announcements in the obituary columns that say that the deceased belonged to a right-to-die group and that, instead of flowers at the graveside, a donation can be sent to such and such a society. Public response to rational suicide has changed enormously in the past twenty years, moving from shock and puzzlement to acceptance and understanding.

The suicide of Janet Adkins in 1990 was treated as sensational news because Dr. Jack Kevorkian, a retired pathologist, not only helped her to die but announced it brazenly as part of his campaign to shock medical opinion into acceptance that this form of death is sometimes necessary. It was a unique event and extremely useful in stirring public opinion about euthanasia, as have been the more than 40 other similar deaths Dr. Kevorkian has attended.

But unless you use the services of Dr. Kevorkian, your death, even if accelerated, is unlikely to attract public attention. I asked a reporter on *The Oregonian,* her local newspaper, if, in the same medical circumstances, Mrs. Adkins had purchased a gun and shot herself, would it have been given news space? "We wouldn't even have mentioned it," he replied.

It may seem that there is always reporting of euthanasia cases. The truth is that you only hear about cases that are the tip of the iceberg—controversial actions such as Dr. Kevorkian's or keenly disputed court cases such as Nancy Cruzan's. Take it from me, several thousand cases of euthanasia go undetected, or unreported, every year. We don't know exactly how many because this remains a secret act of compassion so long as the law on assisted suicide remains in such a confused state. Even with his open defiance, Dr. Kevorkian has never been convicted of anything as of this writing, and probably never will be.

12

Life Insurance

The question most consistently asked of me at public meetings and lectures is whether suicide—or self-deliverance, or autoeuthanasia, call it what you like—negates life insurance policies. The law on this is so clear that I know of only one case that went to court.

Gerald Buck was a 51-year-old teacher of industrial arts in Boulder, Colorado, when in July 1986 he was persuaded by an insurance agent to let two long-standing insurance policies lapse and, after a medical examination showed him to be healthy, to take out a new and better policy on his life. But by October of the same year Mr. Buck was seriously ill with cancer of the esophagus. He underwent radical surgery followed by chemotherapy, but his condition only worsened. The patient had a tube that drained fluids from his back, was fed through a chest catheter, and suffered a great deal of pain, nausea, and abdominal spasms. Toward the end of February 1987, he left hospital for a brief home visit. After talking to his wife and parents for a while, he went upstairs and shot himself.

Western States Life Insurance refused to pay his widow the $25,000 benefit on the policy because his death by suicide was within the one-year time limit specified by Colorado law. Mrs. Buck took the insurance company to court, arguing that the primary cause of her husband's death was cancer. If he had chosen to forgo all treatment, as is not unusual in such serious cases of cancer, he would have died sooner and the family would not have lost the insurance benefit. Refusal of treatment is lawful, but if it hastens death it is ethically a form of suicide, although not recognized legally as self-destruction.

The judge agreed with the insurance company's argument that the policy had a suicide exclusion clause with a time limit of one year. The case went to the Colorado Court of Appeals, which upheld the decision of the lower court. If Mr. Buck had not canceled his old policies, or killed himself a year and a day after the new one was taken out, then the company would have been obliged to pay in spite of the death by gunshot.

The majority of life insurance policies have a provision that death benefits will not be paid if the insured person commits suicide within two years. That is the law nationwide (one year in Colorado only). In the event of suicide within the starting period, the company is merely required to return the premiums already paid. The time limit is there to prevent fraud by persons who kill themselves so that their family will benefit. There is an assumption that few suicidal people will wait two years before carrying out the act. The insurance company has the burden of proof to establish whether the insured's death was a suicide.

If you are considering self-deliverance from an unbearable terminal illness, look at the dates on any life insurance policies you may have. If they are more than two years old, your family is safe. As the Buck family experience shows, it is unwise to take out new policies in the late stages of life. Even if you do, consider keeping the old ones going as well. Remember, Mr. Buck's condition must have been developing for years yet still escaped detection at his insurance medical checkup. Three months later he was terminally ill. Our lives hang by a slender thread.

Read the fine print on life insurance policies and see if there are exclusionary clauses relating to suicide. But if they say payment will not be made at any time, this is wrong. The two-year limit is nationwide, with Colorado as the sole exception with one year. Insurance companies cannot write policies that contravene or ignore the law, so take it up with them.

13

After the Self-Deliverance

Some people worry about whether there will be an autopsy after their death. Either they dread even the thought of the pathologist's knife after life's end, or they worry that their suicide will be recorded or even published. On the other hand, many of us are not bothered about being labeled a suicide at the end. We know that our family and friends are aware that it was not done out of cowardice or escapism but from long-held, rational beliefs. Yet I know from my correspondence that some people still see both forms of suicide—rational and emotional—as a stigma. Thus, they want to know about autopsies.

An autopsy is a postmortem examination of the corpse by a physician who is trained as a pathologist in order to ascertain the actual—instead of the estimated—cause of death. It involves dissecting the body to examine and perhaps remove vital organs for testing in a laboratory. Autopsies have provided the foundation of most medical knowledge that we now possess.

Contrary to wide belief, autopsies are not compulsory, but the family must give its consent. Yet if the law-enforcement authorities have any reason to suspect that a crime or an unnatural death may have occurred, they can override the family's wishes. This requirement of consent to an autopsy in English-speaking countries comes from English common law that gives families limited rights to the body after death. Even written instructions left by the deceased can be overridden by the family. This has been modified somewhat in the past thirty years by various laws that allow for advance documentation of a desire to donate body parts to medical science. However, without specific organ-harvesting arrangements, or the suspicion of a crime, the old law remains: doctors must have permission from family before conducting an autopsy.

Until the 1950s, half the people who died in American hospitals were autopsied. Today that figure has fallen to under 13 percent. The rate remains higher in teaching hospitals, for obvious reasons, but is down to as low as 5 percent of deaths in community hospitals and 1 percent in nursing homes. The reasons for the drop are many and varied: modern medical science has given doctors remarkable diagnostic tools that ought to accurately pinpoint a malady (although some studies have shown a diagnostic error rate of up to one-third); the cost has gone up to about $2,000 per autopsy, which health insurance companies will not pay; and doctors fear being found out in a misdiagnosis and then sued by the next of kin for malpractice.

There are possible benefits from an autopsy. Sometimes what seemed to be a death from a heart attack may have been caused by an accident and be worthy of an insurance claim. If the cause of death is uncertain and a source of worry to the family, then it may resolve matters and reduce grief. If there is a genetic disorder in the family, the autopsy might spot this and greater care may be taken by surviving members of the family. Autopsies can find and launch the fight against previously undetected diseases, especially new ones caused by environmental hazards.

While, as I have said earlier, police and coroners can order an autopsy because it is their task to see that an assisted suicide is not the cover-up for a cold-blooded murder, it is my experience that if the investigators are factually aware of advanced terminal illness they will not request an autopsy, especially if there is a believable "suicide note" that corroborates it.

Sometimes a sample of the drug used to end life is taken from the intestines for analysis. Detectives like to know what substance was used. If it was a familiar medication such as sleeping pills, they are usually satisfied. But an exotic drug like curare from South America would arouse suspicion.

If asked for permission to perform an autopsy, you can refuse it. That is a right. If a doctor or law officer asks the reason for your refusal, cite religion (if that is so) or personal ethical beliefs. Some religions, notably Orthodox Judaism and Buddhism, forbid any mutilation of a dead body.

Moreover, death might pass as "natural causes" if the treating doctor speedily tells the police just how advanced the illness was, and that the patient had talked of euthanasia. So it is wise to have the patient's doctor called in immediately after death.

The family should not call the police, anyway. If a patient has been seen recently by a doctor who is willing to sign the death certificate stating that death was from such and such an illness, then the police will not be informed. The period that must elapse between the last doctor visit and actual death varies from state to state (fourteen or twenty days is common), sometimes from county to county. When making final preparations, telephone the Medical Examiner's Office in your locality and ask for details. Often the Medical Examiner is listed under "Health and Human Services."

In some states the medical examiner keeps a list of people whom the doctor has told are terminally ill and close to the end. This is the case in some parts of Florida, where, because of the high death rate among the unusual amount of elderly folk, the examiner likes to be forewarned. If there is such a listing, ask your doctor if the dying patient can be included.

Until we get sensible laws in place permitting physician-assisted dying, it is judicious to have the body cremated, not buried, as soon as possible after the formalities have been completed. Dr. Timothy Quill, the brave physician who in the *New England Journal of Medicine* wrote of prescribing lethal drugs for a terminally ill patient, ran into trouble when his patient's body was found weeks later in cold storage awaiting medical research. The lethal drugs were then found in the body. Dr. Quill was hauled before a grand jury by the district attorney, but after he had told the jurors the full story of the woman's suffering, his sympathy for her plight, and his respect for her intelligence, they declined to indict him for any crime. But if there had been no body to autopsy, he would have avoided that hassle.

14

A Private Matter?

To avoid terminal suffering, some people wish to bring their lives to a planned closure but do not wish the rest of the world to know that it was suicide. This may spring from an intense desire for privacy and not wanting to be recorded as dying this way. It may be that the traditional taboo on suicide lingers, or the person may wish to avoid offending a loved one who does not sympathize with such actions.

Whatever the motivation for secrecy, we have to respect the person's determination and try to come to terms with it. I am frequently approached by people who ask how they can kill themselves but make it appear to be a natural death. My first response is to gently argue that secrecy should not be necessary in these enlightened times. Second, that today there is widespread understanding of rational suicide associated with terminal illness, irreversible illness causing unbearable suffering, and physically degenerating old age. Sometimes my view prevails in the discussion; often it does not.

Can a person keep their self-deliverance a secret? Not for certain. If it comes about, then it is more likely to be a matter of chance. True, some lethal drugs are extremely difficult to trace in the body after death, but they are rare, hard to purchase, and there is no drug that cannot be found if the pathologist and laboratory colleagues know what they are looking for, or run tests for all the possibilities. I do not propose to name the drugs that are hard to trace, because that information could possibly aid people with evil intentions toward others.

There is another category of person with whose desire for secrecy I am sympathetic—the assister or assisters in the justifiable rational suicide of a terminally ill person. They, of course, are at possible risk of prosecution.

In cases of assisted dying, advance planning of tactics and statements is essential. It is important to survey the circumstances of the situation—primarily the desires of the dying person, the nature of the suffering, the nearness of death, and most important the quality of the relationship between the dying person and the assister.

If secrecy about receiving assistance is not to be attempted, the dying person must write the indemnifying notes described elsewhere in this book and have them put in plain sight for others to see after death. If secrecy is sought about it being a suicide, whether helped or not, then the notes must still be written but put in a secure place for use by the assister only if there is a problem with the law-enforcement people.

Police Duties

If there is a suicide note, or if the plastic bag is still over the dead person's head, then the police are obliged to conduct an inquiry so as to make absolutely sure that this was not a murder. They will interview all persons who appear to be connected to the deceased, looking for illness or depression. They will examine notes and letters. When the police are satisfied that it was a suicide, they will allow the medical examiner to take the body.

Some people find it wisest to remove the suicide note to a safe place, take off the plastic bag if one was used, and just call the dead person's doctor. The chances are that he or she will sign the death certificate because of known terminal illness, and cremation can proceed. All deaths must have an official explanation, which is given on the Death Certificate.

If possible, the persons in attendance when the patient ends his or her life should not be mentioned in the will as financial beneficiaries. Where this is not possible, because it is only natural to leave one's worldly possessions to the nearest and dearest who might also want to be present, then make sure that the will was made out well in advance and is filed with an attorney.

If it can be arranged that somebody else find the body,

that is preferable. Betty Rollin, the television reporter, wrote in her book *Last Wish* that although she and her husband helped her terminally ill mother to die, they took care not to be the ones who found her body. If you are asked to be present at a self-deliverance, it might be wise to leave the house after death has taken place. If there is no alternative person who can "discover" the body, you could return later to do so.

In the two cases in which I assisted, silence was my main protection. My strategy was to wait and see what transpired. When Jean died from taking the overdose that I had brought to her, I asked my daughter-in-law to call our family doctor to come and certify death. When I saw his car enter our driveway, I walked out to the orchard and spent time examining the fruit trees. I was "out of sight and out of mind," as the saying goes, but within call if the doctor wished to ask me questions. Apparently he merely checked for signs of life, found none, and immediately signed a death certificate describing the cause as "carcinomatosis." When he drove away, I returned to the house.

Three years later when I deliberately chose to make the matter public in order to arouse public opinion, I sent the doctor an advance copy of my book *Jean's Way,* so that he would not be caught unawares when the story emerged. He wrote back that he had never realized that Jean had brought about her own end, although, knowing her character, he said he was not surprised.

An astonishing coincidence helped the inquiry into my father-in-law's death that I had assisted eleven years later.

When the local police chief came to the house the same evening, I overheard the doctor explaining to him that the dead man was 92 years old, extremely ill from congestive heart failure, and had taken an overdose. The doctor made it clear that he had been forewarned by my father-in-law that this would happen. The police chief's reply came as a reassuring surprise to me: "There was a television program about this sort of thing this evening," he remarked. "It seems to be happening a lot."

The program he chanced to see was a repeat of the *60 Minutes* segment about people in Tucson, Arizona, going over the nearby border into Mexico in search of lethal drugs to be stored for later use. The program showed the travelers holding out my early "how-to" book, *Let Me Die Before I Wake,* for store assistants who spoke English poorly, to more easily recognize the names of certain drugs. (Note: Ten years later, it is almost impossible to obtain lethal drugs over the counter in Mexico.) Neither the doctor nor the police chief asked who I was, and of course I did not volunteer the information! That was the end of the matter as far as the authorities were concerned.

Television programs like the one shown that evening help produce a climate of understanding that helps to protect a person who feels that a moral obligation to assist the sufferer transcends the current law forbidding it.

No Emergency Calls

Do not feel obliged to dial 911 for the emergency services after the death. If you do, the police dispatcher will broadcast messages about "an unexplained death." Paramedics will rush to the scene to attempt to revive the person, and bored policemen and sheriffs waiting in their squad cars will gladly race to the scene with sirens blaring. Law-enforcement officers are attracted to a dead body like bees to honey, regardless of the circumstances.

What must be done as soon as death is ascertained is to call the doctor for a death certificate in the ordinary course of events and proceed with the cremation arrangements. If the doctor suspects something and feels obliged to call law enforcement, that is his or her right, but wait and see. Dialing 911 and reporting a dead body is tantamount to suggesting that a crime has been committed—and it hasn't.

To summarize: If you want the assisted dying of your loved one to be private, think things through extremely carefully. At all times, before and after, act and speak with great reserve and tact. Above all, do not implicate yourself through written or oral explanations that are better not offered. What you consider an innocent remark may be the critical admission that a zealous detective seizes upon. A family in Missouri who had helped a member to die mentioned to police that they had moved the furniture and turned down the heating, only to find that those facts made up part of the charge against them of voluntary manslaughter.

Make a statement to the police or sheriff only in the presence of an attorney. Remember, in our legal system you are innocent until proved guilty and it is the task of the investigators to find evidence, not yours to hand it to them. Say nothing. Maintain the courage of your conviction that this was a loving thing to do. Let others investigate if they wish. Silence is your best protection.

15

Psychological Support for the Dying

Some people want their passage from life to death to be extremely private, the experience shared only with those closest to them. Others feel a strong need to talk about the emotional aspects of self-deliverance and assisted suicide with others, particularly if they have sympathy and knowledge of the subject. As the taboo on voluntary euthanasia has fallen away in America in the last decade, and as right-to-die groups have gained wider acceptability, an important development has been the growth of support groups where people with a need to share and learn can meet and talk.

There are not as many of these support groups as I would like due to the shortage of psychologists who are willing and able to lead the group. Some chapters of the Hemlock Society have them on Saturday mornings, usually led by one of the chapter's leaders who has experience in counseling. A typical group numbers up to ten people who have helped a loved one to die, some who are facing this role, and a few who are dying and are considering self-deliverance. Sometimes the meetings are held at the home of a dying member who cannot travel. Occasionally hospice volunteers join the little group.

The two longest-running such groups are spin-offs from the Hemlock Society of San Diego and the Hemlock Society of Northern California, San Francisco. Other Hemlock groups that have support groups are Washington, D.C., and Chicago. (Their addresses can be found in the telephone directory, or call the Hemlock Society at 1-800-247-7421 to find if there is a support group near you.) Only paid-up Hemlock members may attend, but a person can join after the first session. The person coordinating the support group will need a general idea of why you wish to attend. It is required that those attending sign a confidentiality form so that all involved can feel comfortable discussing highly personal matters in front of others without the danger of these matters being turned into public gossip.

These are informal meetings, with no agenda of course. Typically, a few people start by sharing their sorrow at the recent loss of family or friend, then the meeting develops into a talk about a recent loss in a family or of a friend. The group moves on to exploring feelings about confronting one's own death. Often there is talk about the problems of coping with the health care system and its expense, as well as exploring alternatives to traditional medicine. The ways to keep up one's spirits when terminally ill are frequently discussed.

As one attendee put it to me: "It makes me feel better to be able to talk with people who are also really focused, and not afraid to talk openly about death and dying." Even in the face of the impending end, members of such groups often feel relief and delight at taking back some control over their lives. Sally Troy, who has organized in San Diego the longest-running support group of this type in America, says: "People experience a sense of relief at their first visit to the group. They meet people they can relate to and there's a bond that forms within the group. Those with terminal illnesses go away feeling much better about themselves. Their day is better because they've been to the group."

Persons who are suicidal because of depression, mental illness, or other kinds of emotional disturbance are not appropriate for this type of group, so they are referred elsewhere for the special kind of help they need. Outside speakers are not used; this type of meeting involves purely kindred spirits talking together about their common problems.

While victims of AIDS often have their own support groups, they find it difficult to talk about the more controversial subject of self-deliverance at their meetings, but can more easily do so at Hemlock support groups. "They feel empowered," says Sally Shute, who facilitates the San Francisco Hemlock support group. "They are beyond denial and are going to take control and make their own decisions. Our group makes this easier."

Discussion about methods of taking one's life is not per-mitted, since this could possibly infringe the law, and, any-way, the focus of the meeting is purely on the psychological and spiritual aspects of accelerated dying. But the tough realities of dealing with dying are not shirked, and many people learn from hearing the experiences of others.

In its guidance document for such support groups, the Hemlock Society says the expected outcome is this:

"Members to become confident about making autono-mous, informed end-of-life decisions that are in line with their values; members to feel reasonably comfortable about their planning for a death over which they have maximum control; diminished fear and anxiety of members about dy-ing; resolution of family issues by family members."

Basically, it is a way to meet people who think like you on this subject and have similar troubles of their own, and for you to feel that you are not alone in this struggle.

Private Therapy

If you or someone you love is facing death and it is causing you great anguish, it may be advisable to seek help from a therapist if a support group such as those I have just mentioned either is not available or does not appeal to you. A therapist who defines himself or herself as a "family therapist" is most likely to be able to counsel on problems of dying, but be sure to make your need known when you arrange the first appointment.

WARNING: Be cautious about telling any little-known health professional—doctor, nurse, therapist—that you are planning suicide. The law in many places requires health professionals to report cases of planned suicide. I have heard of the odd case where dying people talked of future self-deliverance a bit too boldly and the health professional committed them to a psychiatric ward for assessment. Several days forcibly kept in such a ward can be a devastating experience.

Unless you are very sure that the therapist to whom you are talking is sympathetic to justifiable euthanasia, feel your way forward extremely slowly and avoid "red flag" words like "suicide" and "kill myself." Use more gentle, euphemistic terms because, after all, what you are planning is not suicide in the usual sense of the word, but a thoughtful, accelerated death to avoid further suffering from a physical disease. Initially, speak of "not intending to suffer to the end" and of "self-deliverance." The purpose in our language of euphemisms is to be able to communicate serious matters in a gentle way.

Most health professionals today are sensitive to carefully expressed feelings on euthanasia, but there is the occasional physician, nurse, or mental health worker who is ethically opposed and will rigidly apply the letter of the law that allows states to try to prevent suicide.

If you are hurting and feel that to talk about it might help, seek good professional counseling, but at the outset do not be too frank about your intentions.

16

Letters to Be Written

After your death, one or more letters should be found beside your body. You may also want to mail letters to personal friends telling them what you are doing and why, asking them to understand your motives.

The most important letter is what has historically been called "the suicide note." It should be entirely in your own handwriting and clearly state why you are taking your life, that you accept sole responsibility for the act, and that nobody else persuaded or helped you. In the event that you are discovered before death has taken place, you must state clearly in this letter that you are not to be disturbed and want to be allowed to die as intended. Using the law of informed consent, you cannot be touched or treated without your permission. If you were revived you could, technically, sue for battery.

Some people go to the extreme of having the words "Do Not Resuscitate" tattooed on their chests, but I think it is adequate to leave, as well as the statement in the letter, a postcard at your side with the large printed "DNR" words and your signature and date. One man I know sells T-shirts with "Do Not Resuscitate" in bold print, but I am not sure this would be noticed on a deathbed. The garments are more a statement of principle than an instruction. "Medic-alert" bracelets are another warning measure that some practical people use.

Attach to the letter copies of your Living Will and your Durable Power of Attorney for Health Care. These have no direct legal bearing on your self-deliverance, but they are good evidence of advance thinking and planning, helping to eradicate any suspicion of a hasty, ill-considered suicide. Refer to the existence of these advance directives in your final note.

Your last letter—preferably handwritten, not typed—and signed and dated, could be cast broadly in the following terms:

I have decided to end my life because the continued suffering from...............disease is unbearable to me. I consider I have lived a full and useful life, but I now no longer wish it to continue. I have made use of all medical treatments and care that are acceptable to me.

This decision is known to others, but the final decision has been mine alone in a normal state of mind. I am a supporter of ....*right-to-die society and I agree with its credo. I have read the book* Final Exit. *I have made the choice to die now. No one persuaded or helped me.*

My Living Will and Durable Power of Attorney for Health Care are attached to this letter as evidence of my carefully considered wishes with regard to my death.

If I am discovered before I have stopped breathing, I forbid anyone, including doctors and paramedics, to attempt to revive me. If I am revived against my wishes, I shall sue anyone who aided this.

Signed...............................Dated..............

Print name...............................

Make two copies of this note, because the police or coroner, if they become involved, will take the top copy and your survivors and your attorney will need a copy also. It is a good idea to mail one copy to your attorney before ending your life.

Consideration for Others

If family circumstances unfortunately oblige you to end your life in a hospital or a motel, it is gracious to leave a note apologizing for the shock and inconvenience to the staff. I have also heard of individuals leaving a generous tip to the motel staff to compensate them for the disturbance caused.

In your letters to loved ones reporting that you are taking your own life, explain to them that you could not personally say good-bye, nor say exactly when, because you wished to protect them from possible legal involvement. Those left behind can sometimes be quite hurt by not being personally involved and not being able to say good-bye, so a gentle, loving note of explanation goes a long way toward avoiding unnecessary anguish among those you least wish to hurt.

If you are not a good writer, or find physical difficulty in writing, use a tape recorder. Mark the cassette clearly "My Final Statement" and leave it in plain view.

You should also have made a Last Will and Testament, using an attorney, to dispose of your worldly goods and wealth, however large or small. This is more evidence of a planned death. Moreover, those you leave behind will be suffering enough emotional trauma without having to get tangled in wrapping up your financial affairs. It is astonishing how many people do not make a will—legal scholars say about 85 percent of the population dies intestate.

The Value of Planning

As I have said, careful planning is essential for smooth and gracious self-deliverance. It has other benefits, too. The knowledge that you are able to end your life with certainty and dignity will bring great comfort to the final stages of your life. It may even give you some worthwhile extra time.

A man recently wrote me from New Jersey about the struggle he and his wife were having coping with her advanced multiple sclerosis. "*Final Exit* gave us great comfort and helped us to accept the inevitable with dignity and clarity as her condition has worsened."

A woman in San Diego saw her planning as giving her an

extension on life. She wrote to me: "The cancer has not come back, and I firmly believe that an important factor was that I did not have to live with the fear of dying being an out-of-control death. I had 'my ducks lined up' soon after my surgery. There may be a therapeutic health benefit to having the option to 'go peacefully.' " This woman had been diagnosed with colorectal cancer five years earlier.

You will probably need to read this book twice—once to get an overview of the entire matter and also the scope of the information in the book; and once to study and mark out those passages that seem to apply to your particular situation. (Perhaps leave *Final Exit* at your bedside on the day of your death; it is an added piece of evidence of your intentions.)

Some people planning self-deliverance choose a hotel or motel for the act. Unless there is some deeply personal reason for this, it should not be necessary. Your home is your best site: it is where you are comfortable, where the temperature is right, and where the possibility of any callers is known to you. Should you change your mind about the final exit, or screw it up, then there is less likelihood of embarrassment.

Lay your plans carefully. Discuss them with your helper or helpers. Meticulous attention to detail is required for self-deliverance with certainty.

17

Going Together?

Two friends of mine in their late seventies were in an air-craft when it developed engine trouble. The captain warned the passengers to prepare for an emergency landing. "I was very scared," said the man. I asked his wife how she felt. "I felt a certain sense of relief that we were going to die together," she replied.

Such feelings are by no means uncommon among couples married for a long time, or who have built an interdependent relationship. The fear of being the one left behind is constantly on their minds. "Who will look after him if I die first?" many women ponder. The prospect of loneliness, financial shortage, and the possibility of going through their own terminal illness without the comfort of a supportive mate is forbidding.

Cynthia Koestler took her life rather than be without her husband, the writer Arthur Koestler (*Darkness at Noon,* etc.). He was dying at the age of 77, but she was perfectly healthy and aged 55. In 1983 they were found dead in their living room in London, seated in separate chairs. Beside them was a glass of whiskey, two empty wineglasses containing a residue of white powder, and an empty bottle of Tuinal (a brand of secobarbital no longer marketed). Naturally, the outspoken Arthur had already published his eloquent suicide note, but Cynthia's death surprised her friends. She left a note that said in part: "I cannot live without Arthur, despite certain inner resources."

The world of religion and philosophy in America was shocked in 1975 when Henry and Elizabeth Van Dusen took their lives together. Dr. Van Dusen was one of the most important theologians in the Protestant church and he was looked up to as an unofficial American Christian leader. Both were elderly and in extremely poor health. In her last note, Mrs. Van Dusen said in part: "There are too many helpless old people who, without modern medical care, would have died, and we feel God would have allowed them to die when their time had come."

Some elderly couples choose to die together, regardless of whether both are in poor health or only one. It is more likely to happen when both are ailing. Double exits is an enigma that has no scientific answer—it all depends on the personalities and the situations. Such deaths should be neither promoted nor condemned, because they are essentially individual acts. Who are we to look into the minds of others and make judgments? That the couple would wish to die together is a tribute to the strength of a loving relationship.

The eminent philosopher Joseph Fletcher (*Morals & Medicine,* etc.) said: "We should look at every case on its merits and refuse to be bound indiscriminately by universal rules of right and wrong, whether they claim to rest on religious or pragmatic grounds."

With younger couples, when it becomes known that one partner is dying, it is not uncommon for the healthy spouse to declare immediately that she or he will die at the same time. This is a noble loyalty, but a mistaken one. Usually there is a change of mind later. Often the dying person persuades the partner not to make things worse for the family by dying as well, and a sense of responsibility takes over.

I have known people who swear that they will die along with their spouse, but who later alter their thinking and even a couple of years later I hear that they have remarried and started life again. People have inner resources that allow them to go on living despite horrendous personal tragedies.

One couple of my acquaintance found the wife, in her forties, with inoperable cancer. She decided on self-deliverance and her husband agreed to help. But she was horrified to find that he was insisting on dying at the same time. This little cameo illustrates how they approached death in very different ways: One day the wife was seen dancing lightly around the lawn, gently flapping her arms and humming merrily. "What *are* you doing?" asked her husband. "I'm practicing to be an angel," she responded. Her husband ran indoors in tears. Yet it seems that by actions such as these she eventually convinced her husband to view death differently, for after a farewell champagne and caviar party, she took her life with his assistance. Three years later he remarried.

For a devoted couple reaching the end of their lives, both in physically degenerating conditions, a clearly thought-out, mutually agreed upon, and justifiable double suicide is an option we should respect. Neither partner should bring any sort of pressure on the other to "go together." If we are asked, and it is appropriate, we may even assist in a small way, such as finding the right drugs, although I feel that this particular exit is best ultimately handled by the couple themselves. With younger couples, it is obviously an option of very last resort and should be deterred. In all my experience I have not come across a case where it was carried out.

18

When Is the Time to Die?

"The strangest whim has seized me. After all, I think I will not hang myself today," wrote G. K. Chesterton facetiously in *A Ballade of Suicide*. In real life, the timing of when to end one's life when terminally ill can be the most overwhelmingly difficult decision. Nobody wants to die, yet life with an incurable or degenerative illness can be unacceptable for some people. Therefore, lacking a decent quality of life, death is the preferred alternative. But when is the best time? Too soon is to waste the good aspects of life, and perhaps unkind to those who love and need you. Too late means you might lose control.

Sometimes people call me and want to talk about when they shall die. I am extremely careful not to offer a firm opinion, and certainly not a judgment, but allow myself merely to be a sounding board, a sympathetic ear, for the pros and cons of the person's dilemma.

Usually what I hear comes down to two issues. The first is that the person is not at all sure that death is close, but they *think* it may be. I suggest that they have further talks with their treating doctor about the progress of their illness, and ask if there are any other therapies that might be tried. Doctors have been known to be wrong on predictions of time of death, and many are careful not to be specific. Some patients translate such words as "you may have six months to live" into "he said I have only six months to live." There is a lot of difference between "may" and "have," so do not fall into that trap. Talking with your doctor in a thoughtful manner may help to clear up the timing puzzle, because he or she does have a good idea of the effects of various stages of a disease. But do not expect preciseness, because it cannot be given.

When my first wife, Jean, was close to the end with the cancer spread (metastasized) into many parts of her body, she asked me one morning: "Is this the day?" Some people have chosen to interpret that as implying that I was in control of the timing. Not so. The pact Jean and I had made included sharing the decision so that it would be a good one.

Nine months earlier she had said: "The one thing that worries me is that I won't be in any position to make the right decision, what with my being knocked senseless with all these drugs. I might be too daft to know whether I'm doing the right thing or not, but I shall have a good idea when I've had enough of the pain. So I want you to promise me that when I ask you if this is the right time to kill myself, you will give me an honest answer one way or another and we must understand, both you and I, that I'll do it right at that very moment. You won't question my right and you will give me the means to do it." (*Jean's Way,* chapter 6.)

I was Jean's safety mechanism against a too-early self-deliverance. While I did not want her to die, I was willing to take my share of the responsibility of decision making if it brought her peace. Assisting in difficult decisions is an essential aspect of a loving relationship.

Second, there is often an underlying and good reason why people who are terminally ill are not taking steps to die at a certain point. Something is happening on the fringe of their lives and they want to be part of it: a wedding, a birth, an examination result, or a similar life-affirming event.

The bottom line is that they are really not ready yet to die if they are questioning the advisability of it. My advice to people in this quandary is: if you are in any doubt, then do not do it. Make the most of the time you have left. "I prefer old age to the alternative," remarked Maurice Chevalier, the French entertainer, who died in 1972 at the age of 84.

Incompetence

By far the most difficult problem with euthanasia of any sort concerns people who are incompetent. A plain definition of incompetence is: "when a person cannot understand the consequences of what a doctor is telling them." The law requires that every patient give informed consent to a doctor before any treatment or surgery. To do this the doctor must be satisfied that the patient understands the significance of what is being said.

But how does a person who is incompetent (irrational is another way of putting it) make serious decisions about treatment? Or about whether this is the time to have assisted suicide if that is their wish?

This particularly affects victims of Alzheimer's disease, which affects the brain and relentlessly and insidiously destroys a person's mental faculties. "I think I'm losing my mind" is a throwaway remark we all make at some time as an excuse for forgetfulness, but we also know as we say it that it has dreadful undertones.

One person who challenged us all on this issue was Janet Adkins, of Portland, Oregon, when she took her life with the help of Dr. Jack Kevorkian in Michigan in 1990. She waited only a year until the first bad symptoms of Alzheimer's began to show, notably memory loss. She was widely criticized by many health professionals for taking her life when in the same week she had played tennis. They argued that she still had much quality of life remaining. There was no question that she was still physically well, but her mind had deteriorated so badly that she could not keep the tennis score. To Janet, her intellectual faculties were more important than bodily well-being and the decision on the quality-of-life issues was hers alone to make.

Janet, and many other victims of the same disease, are worried about what point their mental deterioration will become so serious that they are unable to think and act for themselves and also become legally an "incompetent." At a certain point in the disease—perhaps after two to five years, but there is no certainty—the patient's intellectual deterioration becomes so serious that personal control is lost and another ten to fifteen years of illness follows. At that point, it is too late for voluntary euthanasia!

The decision of Janet Adkins to die at the time she did probably surprised me less than anybody, because I hear of this happening a great deal in unreported cases. Most of these exits are as a result of Parkinson's disease, multiple sclerosis, ALS, or degenerative old age. I also knew that Janet was a member of a right-to-die group even before the onset of her illness and that she had been making inquiries about self-deliverance before going to Dr. Kevorkian.

There are other forms of senility, of course, and the effect of slight strokes also advises people that their life is drawing to a close. When will the final stroke come? It could be years away, which might mean a nursing home for the final years. Many people have seen their parents through a grim deathwatch and do not wish to repeat it for themselves. It is not uncommon for such people to look back on their lives, count their blessings, and proceed to end their existence. The tragedy is that if there was lawful, planned medical euthanasia available they could have lived many months longer. But so long as America remains in the "do-it-yourself" mode, these early suicides are bound to continue.

Such actions as Janet Adkins's are hard for us healthy, younger people to understand. I have had to deal with the guilt and anger of relatives and friends who cry out, "We loved her. We would have done anything! Why did she have to do it now?"

My questioning in response usually elicits that the upset person knew perfectly well that the deceased sincerely believed in voluntary euthanasia. I ask if they had respected the intelligence and character of the deceased up to the time of the suicide. Once it sinks in that this was the rational decision of a person whom they admired, acceptance of their death, and the manner of it, begins to grow.

I am not advocating that elderly people, or patients with severe degenerative diseases, should take their lives. It is their own decision based on both their conscience and quality of life. It is a highly personal judgment. But I am speaking up for tolerance, compassion, and understanding for those who do make a deliberate final exit. The most important of our civil liberties is the right to govern our own lives, what happens to our bodies, including the right to choose to die.

Alternatives

If I should contract Alzheimer's or another mind-altering disease and become incompetent, I would want somebody to whom I have given prior authorization to arrange to have my life ended when it has reached the point when I am no longer the human being I am now. Put another way: I wish to be killed if and when I become a "vegetable." ("Vegetable" is not a gracious term when applied to a human being, but it has gained a certain earthy popularity among nonmedical people and certainly expresses their horror of such situations.)

I would like to see a law passed that enables people, while still healthy, to make an advance declaration that if they ever become incompetent, unable to make decisions for themselves, then a person whom they have nominated could ask the doctor to bring the person's life to a close. This could be done through a new version of the Durable Power of Attorney for Health Care.

To protect against abuse, many safeguards would have to be written into the law, such as needing a review by an ethics committee, a second medical opinion, a waiting period, and so forth. Sadly, such a law is many years away, because the religious right will oppose it politically and legally. Currently there is a trend in some branches of the euthanasia movement to limit legislative action to achieving physician-assisted suicide for terminally ill patients. In other words, the doctor prescribes lethal drugs and the patient has the responsibility of taking them. But I believe we should have this procedure available as well as voluntary euthanasia (death by lethal injection) for those patients so sick that they cannot take drugs themselves. To abandon those patients most in need of help seems to me to be callous. I would also include both forms of assisted dying for the irreversibly ill who are suffering unbearably and want to die. All the foregoing procedures must be entirely voluntary—and documented as being so—on the part of the patient and the medical staff.

The differences in the ways we die vary enormously and there is no simple, fixed solution for a good death, any more than there is a fixed formula for a good life. Take these contrasts: It was relatively easy for me, philosophically, to help my wife Jean to die because she was rational in her request. The onus was on her. But Roswell Gilbert in Florida in 1985 was faced with an incompetent wife (she had Alzheimer's and osteoporosis) begging to die. Thus he felt obliged and justified, after forty-five years of marriage, to act on her behalf. He shot Emily and received twenty-five years' imprisonment, of which he served five before the sentence was commuted.

The empathy that most of the public expressed for the "my time to die is now" decision of Janet Adkins is one illustration of the deep concern many have about the fate of incompetent patients, and those thousands lying in nursing homes, a mere wreck of their former selves, some of whom would rather die. We should offer these patients a better alternative than the medical hell to which they are consigned, an alternative that would enable them to live right up to the extent of their life's potential, and then choose to die with certainty and dignity when the time is right for them.

19

How Do You Get the "Magic Pills"?

The most difficult question after deciding when is the right time to die, is where to get the drugs that will work quickly and painlessly. It is not as simple as some people think. For instance, one woman wrote this note to me: "I enclose two dollars. Please send one pill for me and one for my friend Mary."

But, take heart, now that assisted suicide is more talked about, and has been the favorable subject of citizens' ballot initiatives, appeal court decisions, and legislative action, it is not as difficult as it used to be. A great many of our best physicians believe it is sometimes justifiable to prescribe the drugs necessary for suicide. Physician-assisted suicide may not be legal—yet—but we have achieved moral acceptance by the bulk of society.

Some doctors just will not help. They are either against such assistance in dying on ethical or religious grounds, or are afraid of the law, which currently is a confusing mess. But around 50 percent of doctors, especially the younger ones, broadly favor assisted suicide. There is a range of circumstances in which they will and will not help.

Who Will

Doctors are likely to help a patient
- suffering from cancer, AIDS, or another terminal illness
- with illness in an advanced terminal state
- where the final stages of the illness are known to be painful and distressing
- who has undergone all medical treatments that are acceptable
- who is well-known to the doctor, and there is mutual respect for each other as human beings
- has read *Final Exit* and talks about self-deliverance in a calm and rational way
- who appears to have family approval for accelerated death, or has no visible family
- who will be discreet about the doctor's involvement

Who Won't

Doctors are not likely to write lethal prescriptions for patients

- if they are currently healthy or their illness is in an early stage
- there are more medical treatments that could reasonably be tried
- who appear not to have thought the matter through well
- whose family seem to be against or divided on self-deliverance
- whom the doctor does not know well
- about whose discretion the doctor is uncertain

If you meet the criteria for the doctors who might write a prescription for a lethal drug, definitely ask him or her. You might be pleasantly surprised. The biggest mistake is to jump to the conclusion that your doctor is unalterably opposed to the concept of euthanasia. I find that, with many people who talk to me on this subject, they are afraid to ask their doctor. But, given the confused state of the law, doctors naturally "play their cards close to their chest," saying little but often "coming up trumps" with the right prescription for Seconal or Nembutal.

A friend of mine with a terminal diagnosis flew to Mexico and purchased Darvon, bought a gun, and covertly obtained a bottle of morphine. She told her doctor about these preparations and was astonished to be told: "You needn't have bothered. I will prescribe Seconal when the time comes." And he did.

Another physician in general surgery wrote to me on his group-practice notepaper: "I have never had a problem in prescribing large amounts of sleeping pills or other medications for patients or their families on request in certain

situations. I recognize that people may desire an escape
hatch and I feel it is my duty to provide it. I do not look
upon them as cheating or lying when they ask me for a
prescription in this situation. I feel a patient has a right as
an individual to take an overdose in a situation of that kind.
I regret that the insurance companies and society at large do
not recognize this."

Alternatives

But if your doctor will not give you the prescription you
want, then you must carefully review your options. It is
always worth an inspection of your medicine cabinet for
any barbiturates left over from previous illnesses suffered
by you or your family. If the drugs have been kept in their
original container—although briefly opened in the past—
and are sitting in the drug cabinet, they are unlikely to have
deteriorated very much. (More on shelf life and storage in
the next chapter.)

Travelers report that Spain, Brazil, Singapore, Bangkok,
and Hong Kong are the easiest places to secure lethal drugs
without a prescription, but even in those places some hunting has to be done. But how often do any of us get to those
exotic spots? Even less likely if we are ill.

It used to be possible, if you knew where to look, to get
drugs without prescription in Switzerland and Mexico, but
those avenues closed off as my extensive writing in the
1980s on the subject started a rush on the market. The
authorities became nervous and closed the loopholes. It was
possible in the 1980s to get Darvon in Mexico at some

small pharmacies without prescription, but in my investigations there this winter I failed completely. Used carefully, Darvon can be effective in self-deliverance, although it would not be my first choice.

Street drugs in large quantities are lethal, as we know from many sad deaths of young people, but the quality is always doubtful. Too often the drugs are "cut" by the pusher to make them go further and earn more money. It is usually the impure drugs that kill addicts, and their deaths are not a pretty sight. So do not consider this route.

Playing Games with the Doctor

You may find that you need to approach your doctor in a roundabout way, using the step-by-step approach. Tell your doctor that you cannot sleep, and don't protest when Dalmane or Halcion are prescribed. (They are useful sleep agents but useless in self-deliverance, except in combination with a plastic bag.) Return to the doctor's office a few weeks later and complain that these drugs just do not help you sleep. Could you please have something stronger? The chances are that the doctor will then prescribe something like Restoril, Valium, or Zanax, which are satisfactory for many types of insomnia but completely unsuitable for self-deliverance. Accept this prescription in apparent good faith—you don't have to waste money filling the prescription.

Pay a third visit to the doctor and firmly complain that your sleep pattern is not helped by the prescriptions so far. When you see the doctor hesitate, as I'm sure you will, mention that something like Seconal or Nembutal would probably work for you. It is a doctor's task to help with your medical problems, and there is now no tool left except barbiturates. Have the prescription filled immediately and hoard sixty in a cool, dry place. Be sure that it is safe from deliberate or accidental discovery by others.

One doctor told me: "Basically, you are duping the doctor. But, let's face it, he may not mind being duped. At least he's not involved criminally, because there was no intent on his part to assist a suicide."

Physicians will sometimes write out prescriptions for the lethal doses if the patient asks by name for a specific drug in a sizable amount. It is part of the code in which the doctor is thinking: "I know you might use this for suicide, but don't tell me." The cautious doctor may prescribe only twenty tablets at a time because that is not a lethal dose, but so long as he does this on three occasions you've got your insurance.

Some physicians will cooperate and even be on call if it is known that the patient is dying and possesses her or his own drugs. The doctor might visit to keep an eye on the patient, checking that death is approaching. This type of support comes mainly in West Coast cities like San Francisco and Los Angeles where assisted suicide, particularly in gay communities, is commonplace. Gay groups store drugs left over from different AIDS tragedies and make them available to the next victim in a private networking arrangement.

Regrettably, there is no point in asking me for the names of sympathetic doctors, because those who do assist do so only for their patients, and even then only if there is mutual trust. With the exception of the brave Dr. Kevorkian, I never hear of physicians who help strangers to die.

Another physician told me: "The person making a head-on approach for lethal drugs may be pleasantly surprised. I myself will provide prescriptions as long as the person is terminal, is my patient or someone very close to me."

Mexico

Americans who live in Mexico, or travel there a great deal from one of the border cities, tell me that it is comparatively easy to get a physician in that country to prescribe Seconal or Nembutal. (As I said earlier, the pharmacies there are now more strictly controlled.)

The method is to go to the doctor's office and pay up front a consultation visit fee of between thirty and fifty U.S. dollars in cash, complain of serious insomnia, and ask specifically for a prescription for Nembutal or Seconal. Explain that these are the only sleep-aid drugs that will work for you while traveling in a hot country. Ask for 100.

20

Storing Drugs

Once you have secured your cache of lethal drugs as insurance against an undesirable form of dying, how do you keep them safe and maintain their quality? This is a great worry for healthy people, since they are not expecting to have to use them for some time because, like me, they think that life is well worth living to its fullest extent. Here are some tips about preserving drugs.

Where

Do not open the container, bottle, or foil at all if you can possibly help it. The original, unopened package is the first and best line of security. If you have opened it, then remove the cotton wool or any other packing; if not opened, leave it alone.

Do not put drugs in the freezer unless you are absolutely sure that they are in a sealed, watertight, metal container—which few are. Neither the plastic container nor the bottle in which drugs are usually dispensed by pharmacies will keep out the frost. Neither will a camera film container.

An amber-colored plastic container is preferable to a clear one because it filters out light. A glass container is better than a plastic one because glass is chemically inert and cannot affect the contents. (Wine keeps for centuries in bottles.) My cache is Vesperax, which I bought in Switzerland when that outlet was still open, and I keep it in its original foil in a glass jar with a tight lid in a dark recess of a closet.

Obtain a few desiccants (those little capsules which contain drying agents) and add them to your stockpile. Your pharmacist will give you some if you ask. These will help reduce moisture.

The ideal is an unopened container inside a cardboard box in a cupboard or drawer at an even room temperature. Make sure that no one else, particularly children, can get access to this poison.

Avoid kitchens, bathrooms, and laundry rooms, which are likely to be damp and vary in temperature some of the time. Most important, stored drugs should be kept away from light, sunshine, electric light, and damp or heat sources.

Shelf Life

The key factor in the shelf life of drugs is how fresh they were when received by you from the pharmacist. Has it been sitting in a pharmaceutical warehouse for years? Or on the druggist's shelf for a long period?

If a drug a pharmacist has purchased is dated to be used by the end of the month, and it is expected to be used for treatment purpose by about that time, the pharmacist is legally entitled to sell it. *Therefore, when you are buying your intended lethal dose, be particular to ask the exact expiration date of the drug you are getting.* The container will almost certainly not give it, but the dispensing pharmacist will know. Do not accept a date one year from the date dispensed.

As a general rule, drugs carefully stored in the manner I have described earlier in this chapter will keep for five years before any deterioration sets in. The U.S. Food and Drug Administration tends to shorten shelf-life periods rather than lengthen them to protect the innocent customer from inferior products.

Even after five years, most deterioration in a well-stored drug will be slight. *To compensate for the passage of time and the shortfall in toxicity, add one extra capsule or tablet to every ten of the recommended lethal dose.*

When the CBS television program *60 Minutes* did a segment on right-to-die advocates in Tucson, Arizona, who were going over the border into Mexico armed with my earlier "how-to" book, *Let Me Die Before I Wake,* and purchasing drugs for storage, they featured a member who kept her "insurance" in a hatbox in her closet. I thought this was excellent advice.

Unfortunately, that program, together with an ABC-TV movie of the week, *When the Time Comes,* gave an impression that drugs available only by prescription in the United States could be easily purchased over the counter in Mexico. It was never that easy, and worst of all, that publicity set off a stream of visitors in search of drugs. The Mexican authorities have subsequently begun to clamp down on non-prescription drug sales.

21

Death in the Family Car

Thousands of people have taken their own lives using the exhaust of motor vehicles since they became widely available in the 1920s. Reports of such successful suicides appear constantly in newspapers. What is not so well reported, if at all, are the failed attempts, their consequences, and effects on others.

It is the carbon monoxide (CO) in the exhaust fumes that is the killer. The gas prevents the hemoglobin in the blood from delivering oxygen to the cells of the body. Lack of oxygen inexorably weakens the body, leading to gradual unconsciousness, then death. Close to 10,000 people in America die every year from the effects of carbon monoxide poisoning, which in the vast majority of cases has got to them accidentally from leaking furnaces or from exhaust fumes from either a vehicle or a gas-powered tool.

Carbon monoxide is colorless, tasteless, odorless, and nonirritating, so its presence is hard to detect. A terrible example of its silent lethality occurred in Colorado in 1993 when five members of a family died in their sleep because a van parked in the garage had been left with the engine running. The door into the home was closed, but the gas found its way through surrounding cracks.

So obviously vehicle exhaust fumes are a way to kill oneself. It appeals to some people because they can just go out into the garage, sit in the car, switch on the engine, and over an indeterminate period (and there's the puzzle) fall asleep and die. An intense dose of carbon monoxide will bring about death within one or two hours. But before you decide on this form of self-deliverance, consider the hazards:

- modern cars have catalytic converters that filter out most of the carbon monoxide (Ford says its new Mustang sports cars emit almost none), and thus the period of inhalation from "thin" gas will be much longer.
- the engine may stop running and you are left half dead. A man in Oregon knew this and started the two cars in his garage; one stopped running, but the other killed him.
- how long it takes will also depend on the size of the garage, the capacity and age of the engine, and whether or not a hose is securely connected from the exhaust tail in through a window. These connections

are notorious for coming apart and foiling suicide attempts.

- during the several hours it will take to bring about death, the chance of a caller coming into the garage is extremely high. The caller will almost certainly stop the attempt.
- if the person in the car is already dying, then upon resuscitation brain damage is virtually certain. This will result in slight or serious physical and mental impairment.
- there is a possibility of an explosion, hurting others. Switching an electric light on has, in certain circumstances, been the ignition.
- the deadly gas may seep into the house or the home next door, endangering others.

I hope you will agree with me that, after weighing all the things that can go wrong with using the vehicle-exhaust self-destruction method, this is *not a good way to die*. The possibility of failure is too high and the risk to others too great. The way of a true believer in voluntary euthanasia is with drugs in the company of loved ones.

22

Self-Deliverance Using a Plastic Bag

If a person with advanced terminal illness has decided to die because of unrelieved suffering, the treating physician should first be approached for assistance in death. If this meets with refusal, other physicians should be tried. Absent a physician's help, a dying person may choose to achieve the end by the method described here.

Take time before coming to a final decision. Discuss the idea with those closest to you, including health professionals, but especially your spouse or closest offspring. Act only when absolutely necessary. If you are depressed, tell your physician, and ask for treatment.

End your life with the plastic bag only if you are absolutely *sure that this particular method is right for you.* Do NOT ask a friend to put a plastic bag over your head if and when the pills you have taken do not work. That delayed action often becomes messy and fails. It is also an unpleasant emotional experience for your helper and might get them in trouble with the law.

Materials Needed

Get two elastic bands just big enough to stretch over the head and sit firmly around the neck.

Purchase a cheap paper painter's mask from a local hardware store.

Either purchase an ice bag from a drugstore or put two wet washcloths in the refrigerator for several hours so that they emerge cold but limp.

Find a clear plastic bag just big enough to go over the head and then be secured by elastic bands below the Adam's apple. Some persons may prefer a larger bag (which works more slowly and may be more comfortable) or an opaque bag obscuring vision.

The best size is about 19″ by 23″, which can be found in the "Foils and Wraps" aisle of a supermarket (often marketed as "Oven bags," turkey size, 19″ by 23½″). This size bag is long enough to tuck under the elastic bands, with space to spare for the painter's mask and ice bag.

Select your sleep aids (such as Dalmane, Halcion, or Sominex) and take enough to put you to sleep in as short a time as possible (at least ten minutes), but no longer than thirty. Over-the-counter sleep aids will suffice if they work for you and are taken in sufficient quantity.

Essential Testing and Experimentation

Well before the time of the intended self-deliverance, when thinking clearly, and in the company of any person who is supporting your action:

Examine the bag for possible holes. Blow into it. Put one bag inside another if doubtful.

Don the painter's mask. This will stop the plastic bag from being sucked into the mouth and nostrils.

Put the two elastic bands around the neck to check size and tightness. They must not be so tight as to be uncomfortable or so loose as to allow leaks.

Don the plastic bag for less than a minute, arrange the elastic bands to be comfortable yet with the bag airtight, and then take it off. You will be surprised how a few quick practice attempts help you become acclimatized to a strange procedure and often remove the discomfort.

Now make a decision about the size, shape, and color of the bag. If you select a larger one, you must be willing to allow the self-deliverance to be slower. Should you be bothered by the plastic on your forehead and eyes, wear a hat with a stiff brim, such as a baseball cap.

Actual Self-deliverance

If a rational decision has NOW been made to end your life because the dying process is too painful and protracted, and if no physician is willing to help, then take the following steps:

1. If you are acting entirely alone, tell all *close* family and friends whom you trust will not stop you that shortly you intend to take your life using drugs and a plastic bag. Such warnings minimize surprise and shock when it eventually happens—they know what to expect. If you plan to have someone with you—which is preferable—go over the procedure with them.

2. Leave a note saying (a) exactly why you are taking your life (name the disease, etc.); and (b) that nobody must interfere with your action if you are discovered before death.

3. It is desirable to have somebody with you who agrees with your decision, but do not let them help you achieve your death. It is legal for your companion *to be present only. They must not aid in any way; or if they do, they must keep silent about that.*

4. Make a decision about whether the plastic bag will be removed after your death. Tell the person who is giving you moral support what your decision is.

5. Carry out this procedure in a distinctly *cool room.* A warm environment will exaggerate the natural heating effect of the enclosed plastic bag.

6. Get into a comfortable sitting position, slightly tilted backward (lying down is not the best position, as you will see from instructions 12 and 13).

7. Swallow all the sleep aids, and perhaps a few tranquilizers, using alcohol or a soft drink to wash them down. Now act quickly and decisively.

8. Put two elastic bands over the head and settle them around the lower neck.

9. Put the painter's mask over the nose and mouth.

10. Put the ice bag or cold compresses on the head on the back of the neck. This will keep temperature low as the sealed bag later warms up. You should be prepared for a little heat and stuffiness.

11. Place the plastic bag (or bags) over the head and draw the elastic bands over the bag, securing it firmly at around the Adam's apple area. There must be no leaks.

12. With two thumbs, hold the elastic bands stretched out a few inches from the Adam's apple, allowing a supply of air to get in. So that your arms will drop when you fall asleep, do not support your elbows on pillows or armrests.

13. Wait until the sleep aids take effect, and as sleep overwhelms you allow the hands to drop and the elastic bands to close firmly around the neck. Breathing will continue normally. Holding the bag open until you feel ready to go is the key to the acceptability of the entire procedure.

The bag may mist up and water droplets form, but the person inside is fast asleep and will not notice this. Observers can expect to see the lips, nose, mouth, and skin take on a bluish color (cyanosis).

As long as there is no further intake of air, death will follow in about thirty minutes after the onset of sleep and the simultaneous closure of the bag. Breathing continues until death follows due to lack of oxygen. This is not suffocation in the usual sense of the word; there is no choking.

If something has gone wrong during the procedures, take the apparatus off, pause for careful reflection, and start again if the will to die still remains. Remember, it is crucial to have a companion with you in self-deliverance to give moral support and prevent mistakes or interruptions.

23

The Checklist

If you are comfortable with your decision to die because of the advanced and unbearable state of your terminal illness, and have carefully considered the issues already raised in this book that might relate to your circumstances, you should now review the following list and check it off:

1. Be sure that you are in a hopeless medical condition. Talk it over with your doctors one more time. Ask yourself if your judgment is clouded by the drugs you are taking.
2. Are you just depressed? After all, the prospect of dying soon is immensely saddening. Ask your friends if they think you are. Talk to your doctor if you are feeling terribly low, and consider seeing a

psychologist. Depression is treatable with the careful use of the right drugs. It is unthinkable that your family and friends would have to admit that you ended your life while depressed.

3. If the urge to die soon is coming from physical pain, insist that the pain medications be increased or altered. You may be on the wrong ones for your condition. If the medical people seem not to be listening, be noisy. Nearly all physical pain is treatable these days with the sophisticated use of drugs and some surgical techniques.*

4. Ask yourself how much longer you can take the pain, distress, and indignity, both physical and psychic. Make a time assessment of what you can stand.

5. Are there other medical options still open to you that might alleviate, or postpone, death? Are they acceptable to you? Discuss last options with your doctors.

6. Are you so near death anyway that you can handle the situation until the inevitable end comes?

7. Given that you are near death, what is it that you fear most, or seek to avoid? Are there solutions?

8. If you are a believer in the afterlife, is your god willing to accept your suicide as a justifiable escape

---

* To locate a board-certified pain management consultant near you, consult the national directory available from the American Academy of Pain Management, 13947 Mono Way, Suite A, Sonora, CA 95370. Telephone: 1-209-533-9744. Other pain resources are detailed in Appendix C.

from further terminal suffering? Be settled in your conscience about this intended act.

9. Will your doctor help you die? Nowadays he or she might. This is the best way. Do not assume refusal. Negotiate frankly but diplomatically. Respect the physician's decision if it is negative.

10. Do this in your home. Check out of the hospital if it is physically possible. A hospital cannot forcibly keep you, but it may require you to sign a release in which you accept responsibility for whatever happens.

11. Who among those close to you might be hurt by your death now, as opposed to later on? Who might be upset when they learn the manner of your death? Is this decision yours alone to make?

12. Give cautious advance warning to those family and friends close to you that you plan, sometime in the near future, to end your life because of your suffering. Do not disclose the planned actual time except to those who will be beside you.

13. Plan to have absolute privacy for up to eight hours at least. A Friday or a Saturday night is usually the best time because few or no trade or business calls are made until Monday morning.

14. The person or persons who will be with you during your self-deliverance must be reminded that they must not touch you before death, and to be most discreet in speaking to anyone afterward.

15. Draft the note of explanation as to why you are ending your life and attach it to your Living Will or

similar documents. Have it at the bedside. Perhaps leave a copy in an envelope addressed to your attorney. Use a tape recorder if you are unable to write.

16. Make sure that a will dealing with your financial affairs is with your attorney and executor.

17. Investigate whether there are any life insurance policies that will be affected by the manner of your death. Also, leave them in clear sight, not filed away.

18. Give the person who will be with you, or find you, the name and telephone number of the doctor to be called for the death certificate. Instruct them not to call 911.

19. Leave specific instructions, written and verbal, about the way you wish your body to be disposed of: burial or cremation, funeral or memorial service, flowers or donations to charity.

20. Tell those around you the complimentary things that might have been left unsaid due to the strain of illness. A simple "I'm very grateful for all you've done for me" or similar remark goes a long way to comfort those you will leave behind.

21. As the time to go nears, be careful about the contents of your stomach. Tea or coffee, toast or a bun, are acceptable. Nothing heavy or difficult to digest.

22. Make sure you have not built up a tolerance to any particular drug—particularly morphine, which comes under many different names—that you have been taking regularly. If possible without causing further suffering, stop using all or most other medi-

cations for several days beforehand to allow your system to clear.

23. Leave the telephone and answering machine as they are, because changes will only alert callers to something unusual happening. Turn the bell down or put a blanket over the machine if you do not want to hear it.

24. If your doctor is going to help in some way, even if it is only to be on call for advice, make sure he or she is on duty at the time you intend to die. A strange doctor standing in for your own probably will not help.

25. Make the preparations for your end extremely carefully, leave nothing to chance, and give utmost consideration for the feelings of others.

. . . and you almost certainly have some very special questions and preparations of your own.

24

The Final Act

This is the most important chapter in this book because, if you have decided to end your life because of hopeless physical suffering, the one thing you do not want to do is botch it. The style in which assisted dying is developing in America is that a person must do it themselves with the lethal drugs prescribed by a physician. I used to think that one fine day this book, and right-to-die societies, could be scrapped because doctors would be able to directly and honestly help people. I was too optimistic. This will happen early in the next century. While the Dutch have government and court approval for assisted death both by injection and the oral ingestion of drugs, even in the Netherlands doctors prefer the patient to handle the final act themselves if they are physically able. The outlook in America is even more likely to be what can be called "assisted suicide by doctor's prescription." This is a good first step, but a more complete, sensible, compassionate policy must come in eventually.

No terminally ill person sincerely and thoughtfully wanting to exit to avoid further suffering wants to end up in a psychiatric ward as one of those stereotyped "crying for help" victims. Where I do hear of botched rational suicides, and when I am able to investigate the circumstances, a slipup in planning is always traceable.

The biggest danger is falling asleep before taking sufficient drugs. A woman complained to me that her husband had swallowed fifty Seconal and drunk a bottle of whiskey, but had taken four days to die. I was puzzled. But a few months later she called again to say that during spring cleaning of her house she had removed the cushions from the chair in which he had last sat and found about twenty-five Seconal. So he had taken half a lethal dose. She admitted that she had not wanted to be with him while he took the drugs so she did not see him fall asleep and drop the pills into the chair cushions. Lesson: *Nobody should take their life when alone.*

Occasionally drugs will cancel out each other. It is extremely hard to discover all possibilities without the most detailed forensic analysis of each case. A person's metabolism can also be a crucial factor. *If it can be done without suffering, cease taking other drugs about a week before the self-deliverance.*

Do not randomly mix drugs assuming that they will be more lethal that way. They may or they may not. *The only drug that is suitable to mix with other drugs to hasten death is alcohol, though, even here, someone who has been a lifelong big drinker will not get the same effect from alcohol as a teetotaler or light social drinker.*

Another warning: if your doctor appears willing to help, and offers drugs, check on exactly what has been prescribed. Look the drug up in one of those drug reference books in the medical shelves of a good bookstore. There have been a few occasions when what the doctor offered to assist dying were barely lethal, and of course did not work. Sometimes this is ignorance or carelessness on the doctor's part; sometimes it is a reluctance to help out of fear of possible consequences. Prescribing "soft" drugs gives him or her the escape of telling the coroner: "All I prescribed was tranquilizers." In some states, notably California, the drug-enforcement authorities are extremely vigilant of doctors who prescribe barbiturates (known as "triplicate drugs" because three copies of the prescription are issued, one of which goes to the state's legal authorities for future perusal if ever there is an investigation), but not so cautious about tranquilizers. *Make your own assessment as to lethality. Tricyclic antidepressants that some doctors recommend as being lethal certainly can kill in huge overdose, but are very risky for self-deliverance by themselves.* In combination with a plastic bag, they are effective.

I trust you have already heeded my warning not to use poisons from plants, bushes, or cleaning fluids like lye. If they do happen to kill, it will be a painful and probably lengthy death caused by burning out of the throat or lining of the stomach. Shooting, hanging, and wrist-slashing are also unacceptable because of the mess, the shock factor, and—even more important—the fact that loved ones cannot provide a supportive presence.

How Long?

Another frequently asked question is: how long will it take to die? It is impossible to be specific, because there are so many factors, most notably: degree of frailty, strength of the heart, and efficacy of the drugs. It takes less time and drugs to end the life of an 80-year-old with a weak heart than a person in their 30s with a strong heart, which is often the case with AIDS victims, who are usually young.

I have helped three people to die—my first wife, my brother, and my father-in-law. Helping my brother die was more a case of speaking for him. He was severely brain damaged in a medical accident on the operating table. Our family met to discuss the situation and it was agreed that I should ask the doctors to disconnect the life-support equipment. When I did so, the woman physician in charge of the intensive-care ward said: "Mr. Humphry, we were just waiting for you to ask." My brother died peacefully four hours later.

My wife, Jean, had metastasized cancer, and my father-in-law, who was 92, had congestive heart failure. Jean died in 1975 within fifty minutes of taking a combination of Seconal and codeine. My father-in-law died in 1986 within twenty minutes by ingesting Vesperax (secobarbital and brallobarbital). The difference in the time each took to die was a result of my experience in practical euthanasia. At the time Jean wanted to die I had no knowledge of the subject and no literature to study. We made no allowances for the contents of the stomach and she took no antiemetic to stop vomiting. Thirty minutes after taking the drugs she vomited some of them, much to my consternation. Fortunately, she retained enough in her system and died twenty minutes later. Eleven years later when I was next called upon to help a loved one die I was more knowledgeable; thus death was swift, without complications.

Without the direct help of a doctor, which is unlikely but not impossible, there are only three commonsense ways for self-deliverance from hopeless physical suffering:

1. With powerful barbiturate drugs such as a secobarbital (Seconal or Tuinal) or pentobarbital (Nembutal). If you are lucky enough to have a choice, pick Nembutal, because it absorbs into the system faster.
2. With barbiturate drugs such as those just mentioned, plus a plastic bag to be quick and absolutely sure. (My personal choice.)
3. With nonprescription sleep aids—ten or twenty—and a carefully used plastic bag.

Ugh! The plastic bag! Agreed. Not very aesthetic, but not so bad with a little prior practice to become accustomed to it, plus careful attention to the details laid out in chapter 22. The case for using the plastic bag is strengthened by the uncomfortable Dutch statistic that, even using powerful bar-biturates, 25 percent of people there take up to four days to die. A big dose does not fail, but, for reasons even the Dutch cannot exactly figure out, some people just take longer to die. Everyone's metabolism is different and distinct, and absorption of the drugs into the bloodstream can depend on the condition of vital organs. Of course, in the Netherlands a doctor is able to administer a lethal injection if there is unacceptable delay. This alternative is not likely to be available in America for many years.

The plastic bag technique, properly carried out by a person *wishing to die in this manner,* is foolproof. Death should come in about thirty minutes. But if you have adequate barbiturates and these were taken according to the advice in this book, they will end life, although, as I've said, in about a quarter of the cases death may be delayed. That chance of delay may be worthwhile rather than to accept further suffering.

Portents of Death

Persons assisting in the death should be prepared for either a long or a short wait. They must expect the dying person to *breathe heavily and snore loudly.* This is a sure sign that the drugs are very toxic. In some cases the person will, although unconscious, speak or even open their eyes briefly. If the death is delayed by twelve or more hours, and the family doctor is cooperative and understanding although not present, telephone and talk over the situation. This can be reassuring.

A well-planned death will come, barring unforeseen medical complications, in thirty minutes. Some will take three to four hours, but more than eight is unlikely. As I have said, in a few exceptional cases it may take days.

Calm and patience by the caregivers is essential in all circumstances. As long as the patient is not seen to be suffering, waiting it out is required. There is nothing else that can be done while the patient sleeps. To panic and dial 911 will bring out the Emergency Medical Services, who will, almost certainly, set about reviving the person and getting them to the hospital for recovery. The police will also come.

Above all, the caregivers must be aware that death is not as simple and fast as we see in movies and plays. We have been brainwashed by Hollywood in the interests of "entertainment." Death is often slow, noisy, upsetting and unpleasant to witness. To know about these signs and complications is to understand and accept them; we have to stand by our loved one at this most difficult time.

The Careful Way

The most important factor in bringing about a quick and certain death is the method of introducing the drug into the body and how fast the body absorbs it. Injection is the perfect way, of course, but that is not likely to be available; we are left with taking the drug by mouth, or possibly by use of a suppository.

For the drug to be quickly taken into the system, it must first dissolve within the body into a solution and then pass into the bloodstream. The stomach has a poor blood supply compared to the rest of the gastrointestinal tract; thus, when there is plenty of food in the stomach, any drugs will be delayed there before they reach the small intestine.

When there is little or no food in the stomach, the valve between it and the small intestine typically opens about three times every minute. On the other hand, when there is a lot of food present, the stomach senses that there is solid matter and the muscle remains shut until the contents liquefy.

The faster the drugs get into the small intestine, with its larger blood supply, the quicker their effectiveness. There will be a massive assault on the central nervous system and the patient will die. Drinking alcohol along with the drugs will magnify their effect considerably. Experts say that alcohol can enhance the effect of some drugs by 50 percent.

To get the required speed internally to achieve rapid death, ingestion by mouth must be fast. In cases of failed self-deliverance that I have studied, the patients usually fell asleep before taking a sufficiently lethal dose. Once the person is asleep, drugs can only be given intravenously or by suppository. The exact drugs needed for these techniques may either not be available or the caregiver may not know how to inject, or may not wish to go to that extreme extent in helping.

A person wanting self-deliverance must bolt the drugs. Dallying means sleep and failure. This rapid consumption is achieved by taking the drugs in different ways. First, take about five of the pills or capsules with a stiff drink of alcohol and say good-bye and thank you to those brave people who are supporting you at this important time. Have the rest of the drugs already mixed into a pudding of your choice, or applesauce or yogurt, and eat this quickly. No pauses, no conversations, because sleep will steal up fast.

Australians I have met in the right-to-die movement swear by the efficacy of the drugs being powdered into plum jam (what Americans call jelly or preserves). As I reported earlier in the book, recently an 82-year-old friend of mine, Doris Portwood, decided that her Parkinson's disease was affecting her mentally as well as physically and that it was time to die. She powdered sixty Seconal into plum jam, bolted it, took a slug of whiskey, and her friends tell me she was gone in thirty minutes. She had also, don't forget, eaten a tiny snack and taken antiemetics beforehand. Phenergan and Compazine are easily available and there is an over-the-counter liquid called Emitrol.

To powder the drugs for the pudding, either empty the plastic capsules (twist them open) or grind the tablets to a fine mix using a mortar and pestle, or pulverize them in a kitchen blender. Add about four packets of artificial sweetener of the sort some people put in their coffee. Have all this done in advance of the departure time.

Here is a self-deliverance timetable:

1. Decide which day and at what time you intend to die, and let those know who have agreed to be with you.
2. Have your farewell note and other documents (will, insurance policies) previously mentioned beside you.
3. An hour beforehand, have an extremely light meal— perhaps tea and a piece of toast—so that the stomach is nearly vacant but not so empty as to feel nauseous and weak.

4. At the same time as the snack take three travel-sickness pills, such as Dramamine, to ward off nausea caused by the excess of drugs taken later.

5. Simultaneously, take four or five beta-blocker tablets (such as Inderide, Lopressor, Corzide, or Tenoretic) to slow down the heartbeat. If you happen not to be taking these common medications to slow down high blood pressure, somebody you know will be certain to be doing so and will provide a few.

6. When an hour has elapsed, take about ten of your chosen tablets or capsules with as large a drink of spirits or wine as you are comfortable with. Vodka is extremely effective. If you cannot drink alcohol, use your favorite soda drink, such as 7-Up. A carbonated drink hastens the internal absorption of the drugs.

7. Have the remaining drugs already mixed into a pudding, yogurt, or jam/preserves (whatever pleases you) and swallow all this down as fast as possible. Some people put artificial sweeteners (Sweet'n Low, etc.) in as well.

8. Throughout, keep plenty of alcoholic drink or soda close by to wash all this down and also to help dilute the bitter taste.

It is the best course, in my view, to let the authorities know that you took your life, why and how, so leave the empty pill bottles on the bedside table. This *may* eliminate the need for an autopsy or partial autopsy. Leave this book within sight of visitors.

The Ideal Elixir

If you are fortunate enough to have a doctor willing to supply the proper elixir to end life in the best manner known, show him or her the prescription described in chapter 26 of this book, "Physician-assisted Suicide and Active Voluntary Euthanasia." This is the combination used in the Netherlands to end life when taken orally by the patient. It would have to be prepared by a pharmacist.

Pacemakers

Some people who are fitted with internal heart pacemakers wonder if the gadget will prevent or prolong their dying. It will not prevent death, because pacemakers serve only to maintain a steady rhythm of the heart, not to keep it going. Once the heart is deprived of blood and oxygen, it will stop regardless of the continuing electrical impulses.

25

The Risky Drugs

This chapter will be a disappointment to many. Because barbiturates (Seconal, Nembutal, etc.) are so difficult to obtain due to their being notoriously effective in suicide of depressed people, and because the plastic bag technique is a turnoff for some, dying patients look to other drugs for escape. They turn to the ones that are more easily obtained by prescription for depression, for use as mild sedatives, and for warding off malaria.

There is no question but that such drugs in large overdose will kill. Even aspirin will do that in its slow, vicious way. But one must ask oneself: How do they kill? What nasty side effects might there be? How long will dying take? There is not enough knowledge on the subject to be sure. The Dutch, in the twenty-five years that assisted dying has been widely practiced in their country, dismiss alternatives to barbiturates as impractical. An experienced American pharmacist who has been associated with the euthanasia movement for twenty years told me: "Tricyclic antidepressants are treacherous. They are not strong and quick enough for a decent death. The nasty side effect possibilities are many."

The side effects that can happen with acute overdose of antidepressants (Elavil, Norfranil, Sinequan, etc.) include: hallucinations, convulsions, excitability, and irregular heartbeat. One also has to consider the consequences of ending one's life using antidepressants: why were they prescribed in the first place? It leaves a person open to the accusation of taking his or her life while in a black mood, whether or not that was true.

Another drug commonly prescribed by doctors are from the benzodiazepine family—Ativan, Dalmane, Halcion, Librium, Restoril, Xanax, and Valium are the best known. They are the sleep aids and tranquilizers that have been developed and are now liberally handed out in place of the infamous Seconal and Nembutal. In massive overdose, along with large quantities of alcohol they will kill. But just because a drug is potentially lethal does not mean that it is lethal in the positive and peaceful manner that readers of this book are looking for. It is the duty of the pharmaceutical companies to give maximum warnings about all possibilities of their products—they certainly need to do so because of their inherent unreliability, the so-called "risk-benefit ratio."

Painkillers

There once was an effective painkilling drug called Darvon, which in the 1980s became known as quickly lethal when taken in overdose. The result is that Darvon (generic name propoxyphene hydrochloride, a narcotic analgesic) is not often prescribed today. Now it is manufactured in combination with napsylate and is called Darvon-N. It is claimed to be just as good a painkiller as the original Darvon, but it is no longer a tool for self-deliverance.

Another modification to the old Darvon is Darvocet-N 50 and -N 100. Here the propoxyphene is blended with acetaminophen to provide pain relief but makes the substance useless for aid in dying. The similar narcotic analgesics, Percocet and Vicodin are excellent painkillers but hopeless for ending life. If you happen to have in stock the original, pure Darvon, remember that it is a painkiller and a sleep aid is needed as well in self-deliverance.

Morphine

Morphine is an excellent drug for controlling chronic pain, but it has one besetting sin: constant use makes a patient tolerant of its effects and the dose has to be frequently and carefully increased to keep the patient comfortable. Many cancer patients tell me that they have plenty of morphine and are thinking of using it later for self-deliverance. Because of its fame as a controller of severe pain, doctors prescribe it fairly freely, particularly the liquid form. But be warned: some patients have taken enough morphine to kill an elephant but have awakened after a few days. Their systems had become tolerant of the drug.

Find out whether the drug you are taking for pain, while it may not be called morphine, is in fact morphine-based. Examples are MS Contin, Roxanol, Rescudose, and MS/L. Because the pharmaceutical companies are always producing drugs with new names, and slightly different ingredients, in their relentless fight for a bigger market share, it is impossible for me to list all the commercial names of drugs on the market at the time you are reading this.

Unlike some other drugs, *you can combine morphine with Seconal, Nembutal, and Amytal* to make them more deadly. Amytal is only available in an injectable vial.

Orphenadrine

Back in the 1980s a drug called orphenadrine was on the world market—in Canada not even on prescription. Word got out via the Netherlands that it was lethal in overdose, so it was quickly combined with other drugs by the makers and lost its toxicity. If you are going to use orphenadrine, use Norflex 100, the plain powder only, none of the compounds. Do not consider Norgesic, Norgesic Forte, or Norflex-Plus.

Chloroquin

A very lethal drug is chloroquine (brand name Aralen), which is an antiparasitic used to combat malaria in the tropics. In America a doctor's prescription is required, but this is not so in all countries. Accidental overdoses have killed a number of people by attacking the liver. But it has two flaws when used for self-deliverance: first, it can have the most serious side effects—convulsions, blindness, and deafness are some of them when this drug is taken in overdose. If the attempt is unsuccessful, brain damage is possible. Second, when chloroquine meets certain other drugs, notably diazepam, in the human body its toxicity appears to be neutralized. I know of one attempt at self-deliverance with it by a very sick person who had other drugs in her system. It failed. A plastic bag had to be found.

Insulin

Insulin is another widely available drug used by diabetics and in overdose is deadly. The problem is that it requires an exact scientific testing of the patient to assess the correct lethal dose for each person. The wrong dose will only put a person into a long coma from which they will eventually awake. During that "sleep" there is a probability of restlessness and spasms. Definitely NOT recommended.

Conclusions

All the drugs mentioned in this chapter have the potential to kill when ingested in great quantities. But they also have the potential to produce nasty side effects and/or induce nothing more than a lengthy sleep. I would not use any of them if I should need my own self-deliverance. Today's more liberal climate on assisted suicide makes it highly likely that your doctor will, if you are in advanced terminal illness, provide barbiturates, either in the elixir I have written about in this book, or in tablet form when you must make the preparations yourself. If none of these resources is open to you, and your illness is unbearable, the use of nonprescription sleeping pills and the plastic bag technique is the best alternative.

Drug Dosage Table for Use in Self-Deliverance from a Terminal Illness

(U.S. trade names)

One gram (gr) equals 1,000 milligrams (mg)

(The measure called ''grain'' is NOT USED anywhere in this chart.)

GENERIC NAME	COMMON TRADE NAME(S)	LETHAL DOSE	NUMBER OF TABLETS × USUAL SIZE
Amobarbital	Amytal	4.5 grams	90 × 50 milligrams
Comment: Extremely lethal. Vials only.			
Butabarbital	Butisol	3.0 grams	30 × 100mg
Extremely lethal. Also comes in an elixir.			
Diazepam	Valium, Zetran	500mgs or more	100 × 5mg 50 × 10mg
Lethal in huge overdose combined with alcohol. Not advised for self-deliverance except with plastic bag.			
Flurazepam	Dalmane	3.0 grams	100 × 30mg
Lethal in huge overdose combined with alcohol. Not advised for self-deliverance except with plastic bag.			
Chloral Hydrate	Aquachloral supprettes	10 grams or more	20 × 500mg
Can be lethal in huge overdose but unreliable for self-deliverance. Best combined with a plastic bag.			

Hydro-morphone	Dilaudid Hydrostat IR	100–200mg	50 × 2mgs or 25 × 4mgs

Lethal in huge overdose deliverance. Plastic bag advisable.

Meperidine (Pethidine)	Demerol	3.6 grams	72 × 50mg or 36 × 100mg

Lethal in huge overdose. Uncertain results make use of a plastic bag advisable.

Methadone	Dolophine	300mgs	60 × 5mg 30 ×10mg

Methadose (also in generic)
Extremely lethal.

Morphine	Duramorph amp.; MS Contin, MSIR; MS/ L, MS/S; OMS Con-centrate (liquid); Oramorph SR; Rescudose; Roxanol	200mg	14 × 15mg or 7 × 30mg

Extremely lethal provided patient has not acquired tolerance by previous use. Expect slow action.

Orphena-drine	Norflex 100	3 grams	30 × 100mg

Lethal but notorious for nasty side effects in self-deliverance. Beware of similar names beginning with NOR and do not use. Use only plain Orphenadrine tablets, best ground into powder.

Phenobarbi-tal	Generic	4.5 grams	150 × 30mg or 75 × 65mg

Lethal. Also available in elixir. Slow-acting, so plastic bag and alcohol advisable.

Secobarbital	Seconal	6 grams	60 × 100mg

Extremely lethal. Fast-acting. Close behind Nembutal as the best for self-deliverance. Most effective with alcohol and an antiemetic.

Propox-yphene hy-drochloride	Darvon Also generic	2 grams	30 × 65mg

Extremely lethal. Sleep aid also required. Avoid Darvocet and Darvon ASA as unsuitable compounds.

Pentobarbi-tal	Nembutal	6 grams	60 × 100mg

Fast-acting and very lethal. The premier drug for self-deliverance. An antiemetic also required, and alcohol makes more effective.

Drugs not mentioned above are known from experience to be unreliable in self-deliverance, or to have undesirable side effects in overdose. It is always preferable to use a plastic bag as well as the drugs above to be absolutely sure of a quick death in 30 minutes. Even with Nembutal and Seconal taken by mouth, 25 percent of patients take more than an hour to die, and a few take several days.

These are the drugs most commonly prescribed nowadays for sleep, but they are unlikely to be lethal except combined with a plastic bag:

Flurazepam (Dalmane) 15 and 30mg; Temezepam (Restoril) 15 and 30mg; Estazolam (Prosom) 1 and 2mg; Quazepam (Doral) 7.5 and 15mg; Triazolam (Halcion) 0.125 and 0.25mg; Zolpidem (Ambien) 5mg and 10mg.

FOOTNOTE: If a person possesses more than the lethal doses described above, it would be all right to add ten or twenty extra, provided that the additions are in powder or elixir form. An excess of pills in whole form could irritate the stomach.

26

Physician-assisted Suicide and Active Voluntary Euthanasia

The first edition of this book, written in 1990, argued the case for medical professionals to help terminally ill people to die in justifiable cases. Fortunately, due to three citizens' ballot initiatives on the West Coast, court cases, and intense public and medical debate, today there is no need to repeat these arguments; they are well known now. The case for voluntary, medically assisted death by willing doctors has been thoroughly made in public by people like Dr. Jack Kevorkian, Dr. Timothy Quill, Dr. Colin Brewer, Dr. Tom Preston, and Dr. Diane Meier, as well as by many philosophers and ethicists worldwide, and by this and other books.

The way America is accepting hastened death appears to be taking the form of physician-assisted suicide (doctor provides prescription, it is filled at a pharmacy, and patient ingests it at a chosen time). This is a halfway house, but it appears to be what we must live with for the next five or ten years.

Ideally the law should be the same as that in the Northern Territories of Australia (1995) and the Parliament-approved guidelines in the Netherlands (1993). In both countries the actual technical means of accelerating the death are at the discretion of the doctor and the patient. But American doctors are reluctant to go all the way, at least at first. This will probably come in the next century.

Voluntary Euthanasia by Medical Injection

Without doubt the quickest and most effective method to accomplish voluntary euthanasia is by injecting lethal drugs directly into a vein. (Medically this is known as "parenteral" or "intravenous" administration.)

Here the physician as the first step makes the dying patient unconscious by injecting 20 mg of thiopental sodium contained within a small amount (10 ml) of physiological saline. Alternatives to theopental could be other central nervous system depressants such as diazepam or morphine.

A few minutes after the patient is sound asleep, a triple intravenous dose of a nondepolarizing, neuromuscular muscle relaxant is administered. This could be 20 mg of vecuronium bromide (Norcuron) or, more likely, 20 mg of pancuronium dibromide (Pavulon). In the Netherlands, Pavulon is currently the drug of choice for the final knock-out. It is a commercial derivative of curare, first used by South American Indians on the tip of their hunting arrows.

The best place for the injection is the back of the hand, using a strong thrust and extensive "floodlighting." Some doctors use a plastic cannula equipped with a Y-type attachment to ensure that the two agents enter the vein successively. This is particularly important when very old patients are being helped to die, because of the difficulty in finding a good vein to enter.

Injecting Pavulon into a muscle is a possibility after injecting thiopental into a vein, but death takes considerably longer. If using the intramuscular method, double the amount (40 mg) of Pavulon is needed.

Some patients will die even before the muscle relaxant is injected. The majority will die within thirty minutes; a very few will take one to five hours. Antiemetics, so important in the oral administration method, are not needed with injections.

Rectal Administration via Suppositories

This is a difficult form of euthanasia because of the problems the patients may have in adopting and maintaining the correct position for insertion, and also of retaining the suppositories for sufficient time for them to dissolve. There is also the possibility that the release of the lethal amount of the drug (a barbiturate) may not be fast enough to be deadly.

Because quite a few suppositories need to be inserted to achieve lethality, soreness in the rectal passage is possible. The patient may also fall into a sound sleep before enough can be inserted. And if the patient's body temperature is low, the suppositories may not melt quickly enough.

Clearly, rectal euthanasia is a measure of last resort. If it has to be done, it must be planned by the medical and nursing staff with great care.

Assisted Suicide Using Prescribed Drugs by Mouth

When a doctor is prescribing a lethal concoction to be taken orally, the drugs are best taken in a dissolved liquid, the "Final Exit Cocktail," because when swallowing nine grams of a drug in pills or powder form the chance is high of the patient falling asleep before a lethal dose is consumed.

Here is what Dutch doctors use today (1996) when assisting the suicide of a patient:

Pentobarbital	9 g
Alcohol 96% v/v	16.2 g (20 ml)
Pure water	15 g
Propylene glycol	10.4 g (10 ml)
Sugar syrup	65 g
Anise oil	1 gt (a drop)

The pharmacist should dissolve the pentobarbital sodium by shaking it into pure water, propylene glycol, and alcohol in the proportions listed above. Then add anise oil and sugar syrup and mix thoroughly. Some crystallization will take place, but it is offset by the addition of alcohol and propylene glycol, which also help to preserve the elixir for up to a month. It should be destroyed if not used in that period. This is not a pleasant potion to drink, but the bitterness is offset by the sweetener and the fishy taste is reduced by the anise oil. Some doctors put the pentobarbital sodium in tap water and dispense with the additives.

Antiemetics Essential

With assisted suicide by the oral method, the patient must have only a small amount of food in the intestine, and in the hours before the elixir is taken the patient must also consume an antiemetic at the rate of one or two every two hours.

When a patient has consumed—and kept down—9 grams of Nembutal or Seconal, he or she will not live. But exactly how long before death will come can vary widely from case to case. An extremely frail person will probably die within thirty minutes. Some will take between one and five hours. In rare cases it has taken several days. The delayed-action cases will probably be younger people with a strong heart, and possibly AIDS victims.

In the Netherlands doctors will administer Pavulon by injection if the patient is still alive after five hours, to save the family further distress. But this course of action for an American doctor is an added responsibility, legally and ethically, so it is probably better to wait. The Dutch have found that about a quarter of the cases of assisted suicide by mouth go over the thirty-minute mark.

With assisted suicide by oral ingestion, the family should

be warned of the possible delay, and also be advised of the noises—heavy breathing and snoring—that occur in almost all cases as death approaches. There are a few recorded instances of a patient in these circumstances awakening for a few seconds, and even speaking, before dying.

The physician who is assisting such a death should be present when the elixir is drunk by the patient and should remain nearby—or on close call—until the end comes. One physician I know who helps people die takes a book with him and sits in the next room until the family thinks their loved one has died. Then he confirms the death and leaves.

Dr. Kevorkian's Suicide Machine

The most famous suicide machine invented was that used by Dr. Jack Kevorkian between 1990 and 1993 to help fifteen people to die. He constructed a small frame of aluminum scrap from which he suspended three inverted bottles. One contained a saline solution, the second sodium pentothal, and the third a solution of potassium chloride and succinylcholine. A small electric motor from a toy car powered the intravenous lines.

The patient wishing to die was hooked up intravenously to the harmless saline solution, while the heart was monitored by cardiograph electrodes to the arms and legs. When the patient was ready to die, he or she pushed a button that caused a valve to shut off the saline solution and open the adjoining line of pentothal (thiopental). Within a minute the patient would be asleep.

Then a timing device connected to the line between the

second and third containers triggered after one minute, allowing the potassium chloride and the succinylcholine (a muscle relaxant) to flow into the body. Death generally should occur within six minutes.

Dr. Kevorkian lost his medical license and with it the ability to obtain drugs for his machine. So he turned to using a canister of carbon monoxide, connected by a rubber tube to a mask. The patient put the mask on the face and, when ready to die, removed by hand a small clip that was keeping closed the rubber pipe.

The thinking behind the machine and canister was that by pressing the button or removing the clip, it was the patient who was physically acting to choose death. Morally this was so, of course, although Dr. Kevorkian was an accomplice by providing the equipment, the drugs, and inserting the needle into a vein. Dr. Kevorkian at first hoped this might also free him of legal liability, but this was not the case; he was prosecuted on three occasions but, fortunately, never convicted. By the end of 1996 Dr. Kevorkian had helped more than 43 people die.

Computerized Death Program

After the Northern Territory in Australia passed the Rights of the Terminally Ill Act in 1995, which would allow both physician-assisted suicide and active voluntary euthanasia for competent, terminally ill adults, a local doctor and a computer technician revealed that they had developed a "death machine" that, they claimed, would put patients completely in control of their own deaths.

The computer program called (surprise!) Final Exit, using an adaptation of Microsoft Access, a database software program that runs on Windows PCs, checks carefully that a patient realizes what he or she is doing before administering a lethal dose of barbiturates. Dr. Philip Nitschke, a member of a group of doctors in Darwin who see euthanasia as a progressive and civilizing procedure, says that the computer asks the patient three questions, all basically restatements of the same theme: "Do you know what you are doing? Do you appreciate the consequences?" The procedure can be canceled at any stage except if the third question has been answered affirmatively.

If the third answer is "yes," a signal goes from the computer via a relay switch to an air compressor that pushes the plunger of a syringe that contains a mixture of two chemicals, sodium pentabarbitone, a strong anaesthetic, and the muscle relaxant Vecuronium, a derivative of curare.

"The program and apparatus delivers the lethal mixture as fast as possible," Dr. Nitschke says. "The patient will be asleep within seconds and dead within five to ten minutes."

Like Dr. Kevorkian and an increasing number of Dutch doctors, Dr. Nitschke is trying to put the principal responsibility for actually ending life on the patient who wants it, while at the same time not shirking the task of providing the medical means.

"When I've talked about the issue of a patient pressing their own button, I get a bit concerned if the patient says to me 'I want you to do this.' I wonder if they're accepting the responsibility," says Dr. Nitschke. "This program and machine are simply a way of making the responsibility very clear and enable the doctor to move a little bit out of the physical space, rather than standing alongside them with a syringe in one hand, waiting for them to say 'Go.' "

Dr. Nitschke, and the computer technician Des Carne, who helped him develop the system, are lending it to anyone in the Northern Territory who requests it, and are making it freely available on the Internet. Just as with Dr. Kevorkian, there is no intention to profit from distribution of the system.

From the thinking behind these two doctors' inventions, the new trend in the Netherlands toward physician-assisted suicide as the main route for hastened death, and America's near acceptance of physician-assisted suicide, a pattern of conduct is emerging: If a dying patient wants to escape suffering by accelerated death, then it must largely be self-deliverance. Put another way, do-it-yourself with medical help.

Euthanasia (lethal injection) will be available only for those who cannot accept drugs by mouth, and even that necessary procedure is currently making no legal progress in America.

Last, but by no means least, advice to doctors, nurses, and others involved in helping a person to die: It is normal to feel sad, even depressed, after this serious act of love. I did in my two instances; doctors who have hastened death many more times tell that they still feel "immense sadness" afterward, no matter how compassionate the circumstances. Grief and mourning are appropriate at this time.

Glossary of Terms Connected with Dying

Active euthanasia. Deliberate action to end the life of a dying patient to avoid further suffering. An unrequested death but considered justified on the grounds of compassion. Rare.

Active involuntary euthanasia. Lethal injection by a doctor into a dying patient, without that person's express request, which the doctor considers necessary as the only way to relieve suffering. Rare.

Active voluntary euthanasia. A lethal injection by a doctor into a dying patient to end life at the specific request of the sufferer. Fairly rare.

Advance Declarations. Legally accurate name for the Living Will and Durable Power of Attorney for Health Care, which deal with passive euthanasia.

Assisted suicide. Providing the means (drugs or gun) by which a person can take his or her own life. Common.

Barbiturate sedation. With patient's permission so as to avoid a painful death, overdosing him or her with sedatives and not providing food or water. Death takes one to two weeks, but patient is unconscious throughout.

Bioethics. Study of the moral problems that face modern medicine.

Brain damage. Injury to the brain causing brain impairment. Life-support systems optional.

Brain death. Complete cessation of cognitive function. Life-support systems could keep the body operating, but are pointless in view of "the Harvard criteria," which define the point of death.

Coma. Prolonged unconsciousness from which a patient may or may not recover.

Competent/competency. In medical situations, the ability of a person to communicate with a physician and understand the implications and consequences of medical procedures.

CPR (Cardiopulmonary resuscitation). Nonsurgical massage of a heart that has stopped to try to get the organ working again. Procedure will almost always be started unless there is a DNR order.

DNR (Do not resuscitate). An order on a patient's medical chart advising health professionals that extraordinary measures should not be used to attempt to save the person's life.

Double effect. Giving large amounts of opiate drugs to a patient to relieve pain while at the same time recognizing that these will hasten death.

Durable Power of Attorney for Health Care. An advance directive by which a person nominates another person to make health care decisions if and when she or he becomes incompetent, thus allowing by proxy decision a treating physician to obtain informed consent to a medical procedure or withdrawal of treatment.

Ethics. A system of moral standards or values.

Euthanasia. Help with a good death. Legally vague but useful as a broad, descriptive term for all acts of assisted dying.

Health Care Proxy. A combination of the Durable Power of Attorney for Health Care and Living Will, phrased differently. Encountered most often in the states of Massachusetts and New York.

Heroic measures. Medical procedures that are pointless because the patient is certain to die shortly.

Hopelessly ill. Describes a patient with a disease that has no known cure but is not immediately life-threatening.

Hospice. A formal program of palliative care for a person in the last six months of life, providing pain management, symptom control, and family support. In America there are 2,200 home hospice programs.

ICU. An intensive care unit, which fights to bring people back from the brink of death.

Informed consent. The permission a patient gives to a physician to carry out a medical procedure after she or he is made fully aware of the benefits, risks, and any alternatives.

Irreversibly ill. Another way of saying terminally ill, but also likely to imply a lengthier dying process.

Kill. To deliberately end the life of a person or creature. May or may not be unlawful.

Living Will. Popular name for an advance directive by which a person directs in writing a physician not to connect, or to disconnect, life-supporting equipment if this procedure is merely delaying an inevitable death. Legal in all U.S. states.

Medical ethicist. A person with philosophical and/or legal training who offers opinions on the moral dilemmas that face physicians and psychiatrists.

Mercy killing. Term loosely used to describe all acts of euthanasia, but best defined as ending another person's life without explicit request, in the belief that it is the only compassionate thing to do to relieve suffering.

Miracle cure. A sudden healing occasioned by a deity or a new medical discovery. Rare.

Murder/Homicide. The unlawful slaying of a person who wished to live.

"Nazi euthanasia." Term of abuse used against modern believers in euthanasia, referring to the Germans' murder of approximately 100,000 handicapped people during World War II. Combined with the Jewish Holocaust (6 million deaths), this was part of the Nazi Party program for racial purity.

Negotiated death. A formal agreement between family, physicians, hospital management, etc., that life-support systems to an incompetent person are better disconnected in the best interest of the patient. All parties agree not to bring lawsuits.

Palliative care. Medical term for treatment delivered in a hospice. Measures that do not attempt to treat the illness but to relieve the pain and other discomfort accompanying it.

Passive euthanasia. The deliberate disconnection of life-support equipment, or cessation of any life-sustaining medical procedure, permitting the natural death of the patient. Common.

Persistent vegetative state. The medical condition of a severely brain-damaged person in a permanent coma from which he or she will not recover. Almost always calls for life-support systems. A crude but popular way of describing a person who is in a long-term coma is "vegetable."

Physician aid-in-dying. Euphemistic term for a medical doctor assisting the suicide of a dying patient.

Physician-assisted suicide. A doctor providing the lethal drugs with which a dying person may end their life. Common.

Rational suicide. Ending one's own life for considered reasons, as opposed to emotional or psychological ones. Frequency unknown.

Right to die. Popular general term reflecting a basic belief that end-of-life decisions should be an individual choice. A more accurate term is *"Right to choose to die."*

Right to life. Popular general term for the belief that death should come about only by the will of a deity, or the belief that life is the prevailing value, regardless of medical conditions or desires to end life for whatever reason.

Rule ethics. Obeying the moral standards dictated by a religion.

Self-deliverance. The action of an irreversibly ill person who makes a rational decision to end his or her own life. This term is preferred by those who consider it mistaken to equate this type of action with suicide. Frequent.

Silent suicide. Starving oneself to death. Usually carried out in extreme old age. Fairly common.

Situation ethics. Moral standards as dictated by the prevailing circumstances.

Slippery slope. Theory that the sanctioning of an act that in itself may not be morally repugnant, or illegal on a small scale, could lead to other similar and wider actions that are.

Slow Code (or Blue Code). The deliberate slow response to a medical alert of heart or breathing stoppage that is designed to make resuscitation impossible.

Snow (Slang). Administering heavy doses of opiate drugs to completely sedate a person who is dying painfully. Person dies while unconscious.

Suicide. Deliberately ending one's life. Around 31,000 cases recorded each year in the United States.

Terminal illness. The condition of a sick person for whom there is no known cure and who is likely to die within six months.

Trauma. An accident or incident that affects the body or mind.

Oregon's Law

The electors of the state of Oregon made history on November 4, 1994, when they voted in favor of the following Death With Dignity Act, which permits physician-assisted suicide under certain limited conditions. Known as "a prescribing bill" because its sole task is to permit a doctor to legally and knowingly prescribe lethal drugs for suicide, the Oregon law does not permit injection of lethal substances by anybody. Actions by all parties must be voluntary—medical staff have a "conscience clause."

Ballot Measure 16 had been sponsored by Oregon Right to Die, an offshoot of the Hemlock Society, which was the Measure's chief financial backer. But the day before it was due to take effect, court proceedings brought by the National Right to Life Committee put the law on hold. In August 1995, a federal district judge declared the law unconstitutional on the grounds that it did not protect persons who were irrational from getting assistance in suicide. As this book went to press, Oregon Right to Die was appealing the decision of the single judge to higher courts. A final decision is not likely until later this year. The full text, printed here, makes clear the extensive safeguards that have been built into this unique law.

DEATH WITH DIGNITY ACT

SECTION 1
GENERAL PROVISIONS

§ 1.01 Definitions

The following words and phrases, whenever used in this Act, shall have the following meanings:

(1) "Adult" means an individual who is 18 years of age or older.

(2) "Attending physician" means the physician who has primary responsibility for the care of the patient and treatment of the patient's disease.

(3) "Consulting physician" means the physician who is qualified by specialty or experience to make a professional diagnosis and prognosis regarding the patient's disease.

(4) "Counseling" means a consultation between a state-licensed psychiatrist or psychologist and a patient for the purpose of determining whether the patient is suffering from a psychiatric or psychological disorder, or depression causing impaired judgment.

(5) "Health care provider" means a person licensed, certified, or otherwise authorized or permitted by the law of this State to administer health care in the ordinary course of business or practice of a profession, and includes a health care facility.

(6) "Incapable" means that in the opinion of a court or in the opinion of the patient's attending physician or consulting physician, a patient lacks the ability to make and communicate health care decisions to health care providers, including communication through persons familiar with the patient's manner of communicating if those persons are available. Capable means not incapable.

(7) "Informed decision" means a decision by a qualified patient, to request and obtain a prescription to end his or her life in a humane and

dignified manner, that is based on an appreciation of the relevant facts and after being fully informed by the attending physician of:

(a) his or her medical diagnosis;

(b) his or her prognosis;

(c) the potential risks associated with taking the medication to be prescribed;

(d) the probable result of taking the medication to be prescribed;

(e) the feasible alternatives, including, but not limited to, comfort care, hospice care and pain control.

(8) "Medically confirmed" means the medical opinion of the attending physician has been confirmed by a consulting physician who has examined the patient and the patient's relevant medical records.

(9) "Patient" means a person who is under the care of a physician.

(10) "Physician" means a doctor of medicine or osteopathy licensed to practice medicine by the Board of Medical Examiners for the State of Oregon.

(11) "Qualified patient" means a capable adult who is a resident of Oregon and has satisfied the requirements of this Act in order to obtain a prescription for medication to end his or her life in a humane and dignified manner.

(12) "Terminal disease" means an incurable and irreversible disease that has been medically confirmed and will, within reasonable medical judgment, produce death within six (6) months.

SECTION 2

WRITTEN REQUEST FOR MEDICATION TO END ONE'S LIFE IN A HUMANE AND DIGNIFIED MANNER

§ 2.01 WHO MAY INITIATE A WRITTEN REQUEST FOR MEDICATION

An adult who is capable, is a resident of Oregon, and has been determined by the attending physician and consulting physician to be suffering from a terminal disease, and who has voluntarily expressed his or her wish to die, may make a written request for medication for the purpose of ending his or her life in a humane and dignified manner in accordance with this Act.

§ 2.02 FORM OF THE WRITTEN REQUEST

(1) A valid request for medication under this Act shall be in substantially the form described in Section 6 of this Act, signed and dated by the patient and witnessed by at least two individuals who, in the presence of the patient, attest that to the best of their knowledge and belief the patient is capable, acting voluntarily, and is not being coerced to sign the request.

(2) One of the witnesses shall be a person who is not:

(a) A relative of the patient by blood, marriage or adoption;

(b) A person who at the time the request is signed would be entitled to any portion of the estate of the qualified patient upon death under any will or by operation of law; or

(c) An owner, operator or employee of a health care facility where the qualified patient is receiving medical treatment or is a resident.

(3) The patient's attending physician at the time the request is signed shall not be a witness.

(4) If the patient is a patient in a long-term care facility at the time the written request is made, one of the witnesses shall be an individual designated by the facility and having the qualifications specified by the Department of Human Resources by rule.

SECTION 3

SAFEGUARDS

§ 3.01 ATTENDING PHYSICIAN RESPONSIBILITIES

The attending physician shall:

(1) Make the initial determination of whether a patient has a terminal disease, is capable, and has made the request voluntarily;

(2) Inform the patient of:

(a) his or her medical diagnosis;

(b) his or her prognosis;

(c) the potential risks associated with taking the medication to be prescribed;

(d) the probable result of taking the medication to be prescribed;

(e) the feasible alternatives, including, but not limited to, comfort care, hospice care and pain control.

(3) Refer the patient to a consulting physician for medical confirmation of the diagnosis, and for determination that the patient is capable and acting voluntarily;

(4) Refer the patient for counseling if appropriate pursuant to Section 3.03;

(5) Request that the patient notify next of kin;

(6) Inform the patient that he or she has an opportunity to rescind the request at any time and in any manner, and offer the patient an opportunity to rescind at the end of the 15-day waiting period pursuant to Section 3.06;

(7) Verify, immediately prior to writing the prescription for medication under this Act, that the patient is making an informed decision;

(8) Fulfill the medical record documentation requirements of Section 3.09;

(9) Ensure that all appropriate steps are carried out in accordance with this Act prior to writing a prescription for medication to enable a qualified patient to end his or her life in a humane and dignified manner.

§ 3.02 CONSULTING PHYSICIAN CONFIRMATION

Before a patient is qualified under this Act, a consulting physician shall examine the patient and his or her relevant medical records and confirm, in writing, the attending physician's diagnosis that the patient is suffering from a terminal disease, and verify that the patient is capable, is acting voluntarily and has made an informed decision.

§ 3.03 COUNSELING REFERRAL

If in the opinion of the attending physician or the consulting physician a patient may be suffering from a psychiatric or psychological disorder, or depression causing impaired judgment, either physician shall refer the patient for counseling. No medication to end a patient's life in a humane and dignified manner shall be prescribed until the person performing the counseling determines that the person is not suffering from a psychiatric or psychological disorder, or depression causing impaired judgment.

§ 3.04 INFORMED DECISION

No person shall receive a prescription for medication to end his or her life in a humane and dignified manner unless he or she has made an informed decision as defined in Section 1.01(7). Immediately prior to writing a prescription for medication under this Act, the attending physician shall verify that the patient is making an informed decision.

§ 3.05 FAMILY NOTIFICATION

The attending physician shall ask the patient to notify next of kin of his or her request for medication pursuant to this Act. A patient who declines or is unable to notify next of kin shall not have his or her request denied for that reason.

§ 3.06 WRITTEN AND ORAL REQUESTS

In order to receive a prescription for medication to end his or her life in a humane and dignified manner, a qualified patient shall have made an oral request and a written request, and reiterate the oral request to his or her attending physician no less than fifteen (15) days after making the initial oral request. At the time the qualified patient makes his or her second oral request, the attending physician shall offer the patient an opportunity to rescind the request.

§ 3.07 RIGHT TO RESCIND REQUEST

A patient may rescind his or her request at any time and in any manner without regard to his or her mental state. No prescription for medication under this Act may be written without the attending physician offering the qualified patient an opportunity to rescind the request.

§ 3.08 WAITING PERIODS

No less than fifteen (15) days shall elapse between the patient's initial and oral request and the writing of a prescription under this Act.

No less than 48 hours shall elapse between the patient's written request and the writing of a prescription under this Act.

§ 3.09 MEDICAL RECORD DOCUMENTATION REQUIREMENTS

The following shall be documented or filed in the patient's medical record:

(1) All oral requests by a patient for medication to end his or her life in a humane and dignified manner;

(2) All written requests by a patient for medication to end his or her life in a humane and dignified manner;

(3) The attending physician's diagnosis and prognosis, and determination that the patient is capable, acting voluntarily and has made an informed decision;

(4) The consulting physician's diagnosis and prognosis, and verification that the patient is capable, acting voluntarily and has made an informed decision;

(5) A report of the outcome and determinations made during counseling, of performed;

(6) The attending physician's offer to the patient to rescind his or her request at the time of the patient's second oral request pursuant to Section 3.06; and

(7) A note by the attending physician indicating that all requirements under this Act have been met and indicating the steps taken to carry out the request, including a notation of the medication prescribed.

§ 3.10 RESIDENCY REQUIREMENTS

Only requests made by Oregon residents, under this Act, shall be granted.

§ 3.11 REPORTING REQUIREMENTS

(1) The Health Division shall annually review a sample of records maintained pursuant to this Act.

(2) The Health Division shall make rules to facilitate the collection of information regarding compliance with this Act. The information col-

lected shall not be a public record and may not be made available for inspection by the public.

(3) The Health Division shall generate and make available to the public an annual statistical report of information collected under Section 3.11(2) of this Act.

§ 3.12 EFFECT ON CONSTRUCTION OF WILLS, CONTRACTS AND STATUTES

(1) No provision in a contract, will or other agreement, whether written or oral, to the extent the provision would affect whether a person may make or rescind a request for medication to end his or her life in a humane and dignified manner, shall be valid.

(2) No obligation owing under any currently existing contract shall be conditioned or affected by the making or rescinding of a request, by a person, for medication to end his or her life in a humane and dignified manner.

§ 3.13 INSURANCE OR ANNUITY POLICIES

The sale, procurement, or issuance of any life, health, or accident insurance or annuity policy or the rate charged for any policy shall not be conditioned upon or affected by the making or rescinding of a request, by a person, for medication to end his or her life in a humane and dignified manner. Neither shall a qualified patient's act of ingesting medication to end his or her life in a humane and dignified manner have an effect upon a life, health, or accident insurance or annuity policy.

§ 3.14 CONSTRUCTION OF ACT

Nothing in this Act shall be construed to authorize a physician or any other person to end a patient's life by lethal injection, mercy killing or active euthanasia. Actions taken in accordance with this Act shall not, for any purpose, constitute suicide, assisted suicide, mercy killing or homicide, under the law.

SECTION 4

IMMUNITIES AND LIABILITIES

§ 4.01 IMMUNITIES

Except as provided in Section 4.02:

(1) No person shall be subject to civil or criminal liability or professional disciplinary action for participating in good faith compliance with this Act. This includes being present when a qualified patient takes the prescribed medication to end his or her life in a humane and dignified manner.

(2) No professional organization or association, or health care provider, may subject a person to censure, discipline, suspension, loss of license, loss of privileges, loss of membership or other penalty for participating or refusing to participate in good faith compliance with this Act.

(3) No request by a patient for or provision by an attending physician of medication in good faith compliance with the provisions of this Act shall constitute neglect for any purpose of law or provide the sole basis for the appointment of a guardian or conservator.

(4) No health care provider shall be under any duty, whether by contract, by statute or by any other legal requirement to participate in the provision to a qualified patient of medication to end his or her life in a humane and dignified manner. If a health care provider is unable or unwilling to carry out a patient's request, health care provider shall transfer, upon request, a copy of the patient's relevant medical records to the new health care provider.

§ 4.02 LIABILITIES

(1) A person who without authorization of the patient willfully alters or forges a request for medication or conceals or destroys a rescission of that request with the intent or effect of causing the patient's death shall be guilty of a Class A felony.

(2) A person who coerces or exerts undue influence on a patient to request medication for the purpose of ending the patient's life, or to

destroy a rescission of such a request, shall be guilty of a Class A felony.

(3) Nothing in this Act limits further liability for civil damages resulting from other negligent conduct or intentional misconduct by any persons.

(4) The penalties in this Act do not preclude criminal penalties applicable under other law for conduct which is inconsistent with the provisions of this Act.

SECTION 5
SEVERABILITY

§ 5.01 SEVERABILITY

Any section of this Act being held invalid as to any person or circumstance shall not affect the application of any other section of this Act which can be given full effect without the invalid section or application.

SECTION 6
FORM OF THE REQUEST

§ 6.01 FORM OF THE REQUEST

A request for a medication as authorized by this Act shall be in substantially the following form:

REQUEST FOR MEDICATIONS TO END MY LIFE IN A HUMANE AND DIGNIFIED MANNER

I, _____ , am an adult of sound mind.

I am suffering from _____ , which by my attending physician has determined is a terminal disease and which has been medically formed by a consulting physician.

I have been fully informed of my diagnosis, prognosis, the nature of medication to be prescribed and potential associated risks, the expected result, and the feasible alternatives, including comfort care, hospice care and pain control.

I request that my attending physician prescribe medicine that will end my life in a humane and dignified manner.

INITIAL ONE:

_____ I have informed my family of my decision and taken their opinions into consideration.

_____ I have decided not to inform my family of my decision.

_____ I have no family to inform of my decision.

I understand that I have the right to rescind this request at any time.

I understand the full import of this request and I expect to die when I take the medication to be prescribed.

I make this request voluntarily and without reservation, and I accept full moral responsibility for my actions.

Signed: _____

Dated: _____

OF WITNESSES declare that the person signing this request:

(a) Is personally known to us or has provided proof of identity;

(b) Signed this request in our presence;

(c) Appears to be of sound mind and not under duress, fraud or undue influence;

(d) Is not a patient for whom either of us is attending physician.

_____ Witness 1/Date

_____ Witness 2/Date: One witness shall not be a relative (by blood, marriage or adoption) of the person signing this request, shall not be entitled to any portion of the person's estate upon death and shall not own, operate or be employed at a health care facility where the person is a patient or resident. If the patient is an inpatient at a health care facility, one of the witnesses shall be an individual designated by the facility.

Pain Control

INFORMATION, REFERRALS, AND SUPPORT GROUPS

• **American Chronic Pain Association,** Sacramento, Calif. (916) 632-0922. Self-help organization for pain patients, publishes workbook, teaches coping skills.

• **National Chronic Pain Outreach Association,** Bethesda, Md. (301) 652-4948. Information clearinghouse, makes referrals, publishes newsletters.

• **American Pain Society,** Glenview, Ill. (708) 966-5595. Professional organization of physicians and pain management experts. Makes referrals.

MULTIDISCIPLINARY CLINICS

This selective list names top programs based on similar philosophies of pain management, though some put slightly stronger emphasis on psychiatry or neurology.

• **Cleveland Clinic Foundation Research Institute** (216) 444-3900

• **Johns Hopkins Pain Management Service,** Baltimore (410) 955-1816

• **Mayo Clinic's Pain Management Center** at St. Mary's Hospital, Rochester, Minn. (507) 255-5921

• **Mensana Clinic,** Stevenson, Md. (410) 653-2403

• **Pain Control & Rehabilitation Institute of Georgia,** Decatur (404) 297-1400

• **University of Miami Comprehensive Pain & Rehabilitation Center** at Southshore Hospital, Miami (305) 672-3700

• **University of Washington Pain Center,** Seattle (206) 548-4282

CANCER CENTERS

These cancer care and research hospitals also have multimodality clinics devoted to pain management and quality of life.

• **Fred Hutchinson Cancer Research Center,** Seattle (206) 667-5000

• **Memorial Sloan-Kettering Cancer Center,** New York City (212) 639-2000

Suicide Hot Lines

STOP! CALL! TALK!

If you are considering ending your life because of depression or inability to cope with life, please call one or more of the telephone numbers listed here. They may be able to help you to get through the crisis and return to normal existence.

American Association of Suicidology: 1-202-237-2280. Available 9:00–5:00 EST, M–F. Provides information and referrals concerning suicide prevention. Also provides information for reports on suicide.

National Hotline for Young Persons: 1-800-621-4000

Statewide/County 800 Crisis Lines

Alabama: 1-800-932-0501
Arkansas: 1-800-467-4673 and 1-800-825-6737
Arizona: 1-800-293-1749
California: 1-800-852-8336 and 1-800-444-9999
    San Diego County: 1-800-479-3339
    SLO County: 1-800-549-8989
Delaware: 1-800-345-6785, 1-800-262-9800, and 1-800-652-2929
Florida
    Monroe County: 1-800-228-5463

Illinois: 1-800-638-4357
   McLean County: 1-800-322-5015
Indiana: 1-800-832-5378, 1-800-552-3106, and 1-800-537-1302
Iowa: 1-800-638-4357 and 1-800-356-9588
Kentucky: 1-800-562-8909, 1-800-262-7491, 1-800-221-0446, 1-800-822-5902, 1-800-592-3980, and 1-800-422-1060
Maine: 1-800-431-7810, 1-800-452-1933, and 1-800-432-7805
Maryland: 1-800-422-0009 and 1-800-540-5806
Michigan: 1-800-322-0444 and 1-800-442-7315
   (313) only: 1-800-462-6350
Minnesota: 1-800-356-9588, 1-800-462-5525, and 1-800-223-4512
Missouri: 1-800-223-5176
Nevada: 1-800-992-5757
Nebraska: 1-800-638-4357
New Hampshire: 1-800-852-3323 and 1-800-852-3388
New Mexico: 1-800-432-2159
New York
   Wayne County: 1-800-333-0542
North Carolina: 1-800-672-2903
North Dakota: 1-800-638-4357 and 1-800-471-2911
Ohio: 1-800-523-4146
   Wood County: 1-800-872-9411
   Portage County: 1-800-533-4357
   Lawrence County: 1-800-448-2273
Oklahoma: 1-800-522-8336
Oregon: 1-800-452-3669
Rhode Island: 1-800-365-4044
South Carolina: 1-800-922-2283
South Dakota: 1-800-638-4357
Texas: 1-800-692-4039
Utah: 1-800-626-8399
Virginia: 1-800-768-2273 and 1-800-251-7596
Washington: 1-800-244-7414 and 1-800-572-8122
Wisconsin: 1-800-362-8255 and 1-800-638-4357

OR:

Consult the Yellow Pages under "Hot Lines" or "Crisis Intervention."

A Living Will and Durable Power of Attorney for Health Care

PLUS GUIDE TO COMPLETION

Here is an example of a Living Will and Durable Power of Attorney for Health Care. Since some states may have special requirements for such forms, it may be advisable to consult your doctor, an attorney, or a health care organization for a form suitable to your state.

To my family, my friends, my doctors and all those concerned: Directive made this _____ day of _____ , 19___.
I, _____ (name), being an adult of sound mind, willfully and voluntarily make this directive to be followed if I become incapable of participating in decisions regarding my medical treatment.

1. If at any time I should have an incurable or irreversible condition certified to be terminal by two medical doctors who have examined me, one of whom is my attending physician, or when use of life-sustaining treatment would only serve to artificially prolong the moment of my death, I direct that the expression of my intent be followed and that my dying not be prolonged. I further direct that I receive treatment necessary to keep me comfortable and to relieve pain.

INITIAL ONE:

    ____ I would like life-sustaining treatment, including artificial nutrition and hydration, to be withdrawn or withheld.

    ____ I would like life-sustaining treatment withdrawn or withheld, but artificial nutrition and hydration continued.

Additional Instructions[1]: _____

_____

2. I appoint _____ , residing at _____ , as my agent, to make medical treatment decisions on my behalf, consistent with this directive.

3. If I have been diagnosed as pregnant and that diagnosis is known to my physician, this directive shall not be effective during the course of my pregnancy.[2]

4. This directive shall have no force and effect after ____ years from the date of its execution, nor, if sooner, after revocation by me either orally or in writing.[3]

5. I understand the full importance of this directive and am emotionally and mentally competent to make this living will.

Signed _____

City, County, and State of Residence _____

Caution: Check the numbered footnotes. Some provisions may not apply to you.

WITNESSES TO LIVING WILL

The declarant is personally known to me and I believe her/him to be an adult and of sound mind.

I am not[4]:

1. Related to the declarant by blood or marriage;
2. Entitled to any portion of the declarant's estate either by will or codicil, or according to the laws of intestate succession;

3. Directly financially responsible for the declarant's medical care;
4. The declarant's doctor or an employee of that doctor;
5. An employee or patient in the hospital where the declarant is a patient.

_____   _____
Witness   Address

_____   _____
Witness   Address

NOTARIZATION[5]

State of _____)

) ss.

County of _____)

     Subscribed and sworn to before me by_____
_____ ,   Declarant and
_____ ,witnesses, as the
voluntary act and deed of the declarant this _____ day of
_____ , 19___.

My commission expires:

                   _____

                   Notary Public

NOTES

1. Include any related expressions of your intent; for example, organ donation, that you wish to die at home, specific types of treatment you do not want, such as cardiopulmonary resuscitation (CPR) or antibiotics, etc.

2. Many states have provisions in their Living Will statutes regarding pregnancy. If you do not desire this provision in your Living Will, draw a line through that part of the directive and initial it, keeping in mind that in the event of pregnancy, states with such a provision may enforce it.

3. Some states limit the time for which a directive is valid. If this does not apply to you and you wish your directive not to expire, draw a line through that part of the directive and initial it.

4. Because many of the states with Living Will statutes contain all or some of these restrictions, we recommend that you choose witnesses who are not in any of these categories: If you are a resident of Georgia, a third witness is required when the directive is signed in the hospital. If you are in a nursing home, we suggest that one witness be a patient advocate or ombudsperson.

5. Notarization, in addition to witnessing, is required in the following states: Hawaii, New Hampshire, North Carolina, Oklahoma, South Carolina, and West Virginia. It is suggested by the statutes in Colorado and Tennessee. Alaska and Minnesota allow *either* signature by two witnesses *or* notarization.

DURABLE POWER OF ATTORNEY FOR HEALTH CARE

NOTICE: This document gives the person you name as your attorney-in-fact the power to make health care decisions for you only if you cannot make the decision for yourself. This includes the right to see your medical records.

After you have signed this document, you have the right to make the health care decisions for yourself if you are capable of doing so. You also have the right to prevent treatment from being given to you or from being stopped.

You may state in this document any type of treatment that you do not desire or that you want to make sure you receive.

You have the right to revoke the authority of your attorney-in-fact, either orally or in writing. If you do take away that authority, notify everyone with a copy of the Power of Attorney, ideally in writing.

If there is anything in this document that you do not understand, ask your lawyer to explain it to you.

You should keep a copy of this document after you have signed it. Give a copy to the person(s) you name as your attorney-in-fact and alternate. Give copies to your regular doctors and any health care facility where you have been and expect to be a patient again.

Creation of Durable Power of Attorney. By this document I intend to create a Durable Power of Attorney for Health Care. This power of attorney shall not be affected by my subsequent incapacity or disability.

Revocation. I revoke any prior Durable Power of Attorney for Health Care.

Designation of Attorney-in-fact and Alternate. I appoint _____ , whose address is _____ , and whose telephone number is _____ , as my attorney-in-fact for health care decisions. I appoint _____ , whose address is _____ , and whose telephone number is _____ , as my alternative attorney-in-fact for health care decisions. I authorize my attorney-in-fact appointed by this document to make health care decisions for me when I am incapable of making my own health care decisions.

Desires, Special Instructions, Limitations[1]: _____
_____

In addition, I direct that my attorney-in-fact have authority to make decisions regarding the following:
(INITIAL ONE OR BOTH.)

____ Withholding or withdrawal of life-sustaining procedures with the understanding that death may result.

____ Withholding or withdrawal of artificially administered hydration or nutrition or both with the understanding that death may result.

I understand the contents of this document and the powers granted to my attorney-in-fact.
Signed _____   Date _____

WITNESSES TO THE DURABLE POWER OF ATTORNEY FOR HEALTH CARE[2]

The declarant is personally known to me and I believe her/him to be at least 18 years old, and of sound mind. I am not:

1. Related to the declarant by blood or marriage;
2. Entitled to any portion of the declarant's estate either by will or codicil, or according to the laws of intestate succession;
3. Directly financially responsible for the declarant's medical care;
4. The declarant's doctor or an employee of that doctor;
5. An employee or patient in the hospital or health care facility where the declarant is a patient.

_____   _____
Witness   Address

_____   _____
Witness   Address

Caution: Check the numbered footnotes. Some provisions may not apply to you.

NOTARIZATION[3]

State of _____)
) ss.
County of _____)
    Subscribed and sworn to before me by_____
_____ , Declarant and
_____ ,witnesses, as the voluntary act and deed of the declarant this _____ day of _____ , 19____.
My commission expires:

_____
Notary Public

ACCEPTANCE OF APPOINTMENT OF POWER OF ATTORNEY[4]

I have discussed with _____ (principal) and agree to serve as attorney-in-fact for health care decisions. I understand I have a duty to act consistently with the desires of the principal as expressed in this appointment. I understand that this document gives me authority over health care decisions for the principal only if the principal becomes incapable or otherwise disabled. I understand that I must act in good faith in exercising my authority under this power of attorney. I understand that the principal may revoke this power of attorney at any time in any manner.

_____   _____

Signature of Attorney-in-fact   Date

_____   _____

Signature of Alternate Attorney-in-fact   Date

Caution: Check the numbered footnotes. Some provisions may not apply to you.

1. Use this space to note the types of treatment you want done or do not want done; some examples are CPR, antibiotics, respirators, organ donation, transfusions. You may add additional pages of instructions; be sure to sign and date them.

2. Although witnesses are not required in several states, and the requirements of who may be a witness vary from state to state, we recommend that you have your Durable Power of Attorney for Health Care witnessed according to this form. This may help protect you if you move to or become disabled in another state. Your attorney-in-fact and alternate should *never* be witnesses.

3. Notarization, in addition to witnessing, is required in Illinois. Maine, New Jersey, and Utah require only notarization. Nevada, California, and Idaho allow *either* signature by two witnesses *or* notarization.

We recommend notarization of this form, when possible, even if you do not live in one of the specified states.

4. New Jersey and Oregon require a signed acceptance by the attorney-in-fact. New York requires a statement of discussion. We recommend that you discuss your desires with your attorney-in-fact and have him or her sign this acceptance.

COMMON QUESTIONS ABOUT THE LIVING WILL

1. What is a Living Will?

A Living Will (often called a Medical Directive or Directive to Physicians) is a document which lets you tell your doctor in advance that you do not want your life artificially extended in certain situations. The two situations where a directive may be used are (1) when you have an incurable injury, disease, or illness which two doctors agree is terminal; and (2) when life-sustaining procedures would only prolong the moment of your death, when you would die whether these procedures were used or not.

2. Who can make a Living Will?

You must be at least 18 years of age or older, and of sound mind to make a Living Will in most states.

3. Who can witness a Living Will?

A majority of states require that only certain people witness a Living Will. At the time the Living Will is witnessed, the witnesses should not be related to you by blood or marriage, entitled to part of your estate if you die, either through your will, by law, or because of bills owed, or be your attending doctor or an employee of that doctor or the health care facility where you are a patient.

4. If I make a Living Will, is it permanent?

A Living Will is permanent from the time it is finalized, except in California and North Dakota. If you change your mind at any time, you may revoke the directive by destroying it, writing down your intent or telling someone. Make sure to tell your doctor and anyone else with a copy of the directive of changes.

5. What if my doctor doesn't want to honor my Living Will?

A doctor who doesn't want to honor a Living Will is required by most laws to try to find another doctor or health care facility where your wishes will be carried out. Talk with your doctor when you complete your Living Will, giving him or her a copy for your medical record, so you can be sure that you agree.

6. Will completing a Living Will affect my insurance policies?

No. Most statutes specify that insurance policies will not be legally impaired or invalidated by signing a directive or putting it into effect.

7. Where should I keep my Living Will?

Keep your original Living Will in a safe place in your home, give a photocopy to a friend or family member, and be sure to give a photocopy to your doctor for his or her record and a hospital where you have a medical record and would go when hospitalized.

8. Is my Living Will legally enforceable?

No. While it is recognized by law in most states, health care providers are not always required to comply with it. It is a request and of value as evidence. Most doctors will respect a Living Will as a lawful refusal of treatment.

COMMON QUESTIONS ABOUT THE DURABLE POWER OF ATTORNEY FOR HEALTH CARE

1. What is a Durable Power of Attorney for Health Care?

A Durable Power of Attorney for Health Care lets you choose a person in advance to make medical or health care decisions for you if you become incapable of doing so.

2. Who can make such a power of attorney?

A person who is an adult and has the capacity to make health care decisions may make a power of attorney.

3. Do I need a lawyer to write a Power of Attorney for Health Care?

Although you do not need a lawyer to write a Power of Attorney for Health Care, if there is anything in the document that you do not understand, you should consult a lawyer.

4. Who will decide that I am incapable of making my own health care decisions?

Usually your doctor and one other doctor determine that you are not capable of making health care decisions; in rare cases a court will decide.

5. How long does a Power of Attorney for Health Care last?

The period of time for which a Power of Attorney for Health Care is good may vary by state. It may also end if you die, if you revoke it, or if both the attorney-in-fact and alternate attorney-in-fact withdraw. If you become incapable of making health care decisions during the period of validity and the power of attorney goes into effect, it will remain in effect until you are no longer incapable or until you die.

You should periodically review both your Living Will and power of attorney, revising them when necessary.

6. What if I change my mind?

If you change your mind at any time about who should be your attorney-in-fact, what decisions he or she may make, or whether you want a Power of Attorney for Health Care, you can revoke the power of attorney in any manner. Make sure that you let your doctor and anyone with copies know that you have changed your mind.

7. Who can be my attorney-in-fact?

An attorney-in-fact does not have to be a lawyer; he or she can be any adult you choose except for your attending doctor or an employee of that doctor who is not related to you by blood, marriage, or adoption; or an owner, operator, or employee of a health care facility where you are a patient or resident, if they are not related to you by blood, marriage, or adoption.

The person you choose should agree in writing to serve as your attorney-in-fact; he or she can withdraw at any time.

If you choose your husband or wife as attorney-in-fact and later divorce, you will need to make a new power of attorney naming that person or someone else as attorney-in-fact.

8. What kinds of decisions will my attorney-in-fact be able to make?

A written Power of Attorney for Health Care gives only the authority to make health care decisions for you that you would have made if you were not incapable. If you want that person to make decisions about withdrawing or withholding a procedure or food and water necessary to keep you alive, you should say so on the power of attorney. Your attorney-in-fact will also have a right to see your medical records.

Your attorney-in-fact must act according to what he or she believes that you would want, or if that is not known, in your best interest.

9. What if my doctor doesn't want to honor the wishes of my attorney-in-fact?

A doctor who fails to honor your wishes regarding consent to or refusal of treatment may be liable for damages, because you have a common law and constitutional right to make such decisions. Talk to your doctor when you complete your Durable Power of Attorney for Health Care, giving him or her a copy for your medical record, so you can be sure you agree.

10. Will my attorney-in-fact be responsible for the cost of my medical care?

No. Your attorney-in-fact is acting in a decision-making capacity and is only responsible for making health care decisions.

Books to Read

Case Histories

First You Cry, by Betty Rollin. (Signet, 1977)
Last Wish, by Betty Rollin. (Warner, 1987)
Death of a Man, by Lael Wertenbaker. (Random House, 1957)
Jean's Way, by Derek Humphry. (Perennial Books, 1978)
A Chosen Death, by Lonny Shavelson, M.D. (Simon & Schuster, 1995)

Advisory

Final Acts of Love: Families, Friends and Assisted Dying, by Stephen Jamison. (Putnam, 1996)

History and Ethics

The Right to Die: Understanding Euthanasia, by Derek Humphry and Ann Wickett. (Harper & Row, 1986)
Death by Choice, by Daniel C. Maguire. (Schocken Books, 1975)
Dying with Dignity, by Derek Humphry. (St. Martin's Press, 1992)
Morals and Medicine, by Joseph Fletcher. (Beacon Press, 1954)
The Savage God, by A. Alvarez. (Bantam Books, 1976)

Deathright: Culture, Medicine, Politics and the Right to Die, by
   James M. Hoefler. (Westview Press, 1994)
Rethinking Life and Death, by Peter Singer. (St. Martin's Press,
   1995)

Elder Suicide

Commonsense Suicide: The Final Right by Doris Portwood. (Dodd,
   Mead, 1978)

Religion

Euthanasia and Religion, by Gerald A. Larue. (Hemlock Society,
   1985)
Playing God: 50 Religions' View on Your Right to Die, by Gerald A.
   Larue. (Moyer, Bell, 1996)

Plays

Whose Life Is It, Anyway? by Brian Clark. (Avon, 1980)
Is This The Day? by Vilma Hollingberry. (Hemlock Society, 1990)

Novels

Lethal Dose, by Stephen Snodgrass (ICAM, 1996)
Critical Care, by Richard Dooling. (Morrow, 1992)
The Woman Said Yes, by Jessamyn West. (Harcourt Brace Jova-
   novitch, 1976)
In the Night Season, by Christian Barnard. (Prentice Hall, 1978)
One True Thing, by Anna Quindlen. (Random House, 1994)
A Stone Boat, by Andrew Solomon. (Faber and Faber, 1994)

Burials and Ceremonies

*Dealing Creatively with Death: A Manual of Death Education and
   Simple Burial*, by Ernest Morgan. (Barclay House, 13th edition)

Euthanasia Research & Guidance Organization
(ERGO!)

Putting Assisted Dying into Careful Practice

•Information •Guidelines •Advice •Support •Literature •Research
•News Briefings

Address: Messages/FAX
24829 Norris Lane   541/998-1873
Junction City, OR 97448-9559

INTERNET
E-mail: Ergo@efn.org
Web site: http://www.FinalExit.org

A nonprofit, tax-deductible Oregon corporation founded in 1993. Free
brochure available upon request.

About the Author

Derek Humphry, president of the Euthanasia Research and Guidance Organization (ERGO!) and founder and executive director (1980-1992) of the National Hemlock Society, was a newspaper reporter for 35 years, working for many British journals. During his 14 years with the London *Sunday Times*, he began to write books on racial problems, law enforcement, and civil liberties. In 1978 he moved to the United States to work for the *Los Angeles Times*. The international acceptance of the story of his first wife's death, *Jean's Way*, now considered a classic account of rational voluntary euthanasia, launched his campaign for the right to lawful physician aid-in-dying. In 1980 in Los Angeles he and friends formed the Hemlock Society, the first such group in North America. From 1988 to 1990, Derek Humphry was President of the World Federation of Right to Die Societies. He is the highly acclaimed author of *Let Me De Before I Wake*, which is also available from DELL. He lives in Eugene, Oregon, where he sails for recreation.